GORBACH
AND HIS
REVOLUTION

European History in Perspective
General Editor: Jeremy Black

GORBACHEV
AND HIS
REVOLUTION

MARK GALEOTTI
Lecturer in International History
University of Keele

First published 1997 by
MACMILLAN PRESS LTD
Houndmills, Basingstoke, Hampshire RG21 6XS
and London
Companies and representatives
throughout the world

ISBN 0–333–63854–9 hardcover
ISBN 0–333–63855–7 paperback

A catalogue record for this book is available
from the British Library

This book is printed on paper suitable for recycling and
made from fully managed and sustained forest sources.

10 9 8 7 6 5 4 3 2 1
06 05 04 03 02 01 00 99 98 97

Formatted by **CJB EDITORIAL PLUS**
Printed in Hong Kong

Published in the United States of America 1997 by
ST. MARTIN'S PRESS, INC.,
Scholarly and Reference Division
175 Fifth Avenue, New York, N. Y. 10010

ISBN 0–312–16481–5 (cloth)
ISBN 0–312–16482–3 (paperback)

CONTENTS

ILLUSTRATIONS

Figures

Map

PREFACE AND ACKNOWLEDGEMENTS

This is not a learned research work, laden with footnotes and eager to emphasize the differences of interpretation to be found in academe. I make no apologies for that; there are, as I discuss in the Bibliography, many first class heavyweight texts on Gorbachev and his times. Instead, this book sets out to provide an introduction for readers new to the USSR and its final years. Inevitably, this means that often I have swept through very necessary and important debates with cavalier disregard and simply selected the line of argument I felt worth using. My sympathies are with those whose work is thus ignored, but I am afraid that this book does not pretend to do more than provide a simple and readable primer to a complex and much-debated era.

I hope it also conveys some sense of the pace and excitement of the times. My own professional interest in modern Russia coincided with the developments covered in this book, from my first trip as a school-age tourist in the dying years of the Brezhnev era to the research for my PhD taking full advantage of the new openness and freedoms of the later 1980s and just before taking up my present job at Keele University, a trip to Moscow in that fateful month, August 1991. As for so many other scholars of my generation, it was Mikhail Gorbachev who created the enthusiasm which drove me into study of modern Russia. My only hope is that I can conjure up some of that same sense of history being made for a new generation of students. To do this, I have concentrated upon Gorbachev himself. In some ways, this is a backward step. History, thank heavens, is no longer defined as the 'doings of great men'. It is about men, women, countries, organizations, peoples and institutions shaping and being shaped by the great, impersonal forces of economics, of society and of fate. Yet to pretend that Gorbachev's own choices and character played no part in the events here described is to ignore the very necessary human dimension to history. Gorbachev took power at a pivotal moment in Russian history, and the revolution he precipitated bears the stamp of his flaws and his greatness.

In many ways, writing this book has been rather harder than other projects I have undertaken. For dealing with my sometimes irascible concentration on it and for helping me finish it, I owe a particular debt of gratitude to my wife, Mickey. Amidst the long-winded and roundabout conversations of academe, the blunt instruction, 'so write it' proved a refreshingly brutal tonic!

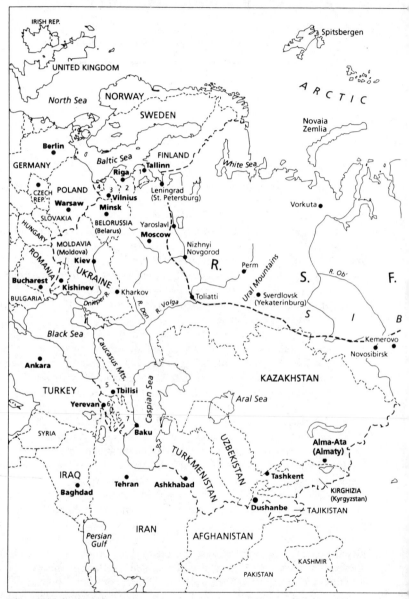

The USSR in 1991

Source: reprinted from *Last of the Empires* by John Keep (1995),
by permission of Oxford University Press

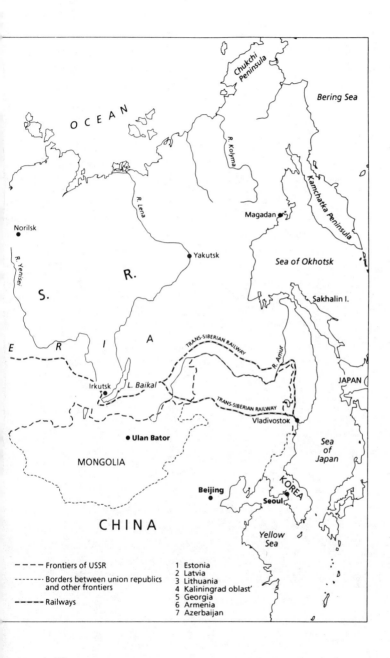

O C E A N

Chukchi Peninsula

Bering Sea

R. Kolyma

Kamchatka Peninsula

Norilsk

R. Lena

Magadan

R. Yenisei

S. R.

Yakutsk

Sea of Okhotsk

E R I A

Sakhalin I.

TRANS-SIBERIAN RAILWAY

R. Amur

JAPAN

Irkutsk   L. Baikal

TRANS-SIBERIAN RAILWAY

Vladivostok

Ulan Bator

Sea of Japan

MONGOLIA

Beijing

KOREA

Seoul

CHINA

Yellow Sea

- - - - Frontiers of USSR
- - - - Borders between union republics and other frontiers
- - - - Railways

1 Estonia
2 Latvia
3 Lithuania
4 Kaliningrad oblast'
5 Georgia
6 Armenia
7 Azerbaijan

1

THE DECAY OF THE SOVIET UNION

The Soviet Union was a country of astonishing variety and contrasts. Generations of Communist Party bureaucrats, planners, educators, propagandists and secret policemen had tried to turn it into an ordered, standardized, logical, controlled human machine. But despite this – or perhaps because of this – beneath its drab and standardized exterior bubbled a way of life rich in its passions, options and energy. The Baltic states of Latvia, Estonia and Lithuania had been relatively recently incorporated into the USSR, by conquest after the Second World War. Their culture was thoroughly European, looking north and west along the Baltic and to Scandinavia. To the south, the Transcaucasians of Georgia, Armenia and Azerbaijan kept alive traditions of clan loyalty and blood vengeance which predated the Imperial Russian conquerors of the nineteenth century and still survive to this day. To the far south-east were the Central Asian Soviet Socialist Republics of Kirghizia, Kazakhstan, Tajikistan, Turkmenistan and Uzbekistan. There the Communist ideals of Marxism–Leninism were forever in competition with Islam for people's hearts and minds, and Soviet power was to prove often little more than skin deep. In between lay the industrial cities of European Russia, the rolling cornfields of the Ukraine, the trackless forests of frozen Siberia. For this was a nation built upon the ruins of one of the world's great empires, the Russia of the Tsars, with a population in 1980 of 265 million and a land area of 22.4 million square kilometres – 40 million more people than the USA and almost two and half times its size.

Reforming Russia

The history of the USSR – like that of the tsarist empire – was to a large extent dominated by the struggle of the centre to impose its authority upon the people and regions of this huge and varied country. Many rulers were content simply to hold on to what they had. Others, though, tried to change this sprawling, backward nation, and the common denominator of all those who were to be successful in stamping their mark upon it was a preparedness to use force. In the eighteenth century, Peter the Great began the process of modernizing Russia. He brought in Europeans to train his armies and build him industries. The city of St Petersburg (called Leningrad for much of this century) was his monument, his 'window on the West'. But to do this, he smashed the power of the aristocratic families and the old army and squeezed from the peasants all the taxes and tribute he could, in order to pay for his dreams. He was prepared to grant cities their own charters to elect their own officials, for example, but only if they were prepared to pay double their old taxes. There was no room for dissent in Peter's Russia. When the Don Cossacks rose in revolt in 1707, he declared that 'these locusts cannot be treated other than with cruelty'. Building St Petersburg was a huge venture, and between 1712 and 1715, 20 000 peasants per year were being dragooned into the project. When they tried to resist peacefully, by fleeing before they could be press-ganged on to the construction teams, the government introduced a law requiring every peasant to carry at all times an internal passport – an eighteenth century identity card! – to allow it to round up runaways.

By contrast, when Alexander II emancipated the serfs in 1861, he freed them from their traditional ties to the land and obedience to their landlords. Where Peter had used force to demand obedience, Alexander – the 'Tsar-Liberator' – thought to win the people's loyalty and labour by gratitude and enlightened self-interest. The result was failure. The landlords and nobility subverted the plans, keeping the best land and selling the rest to the peasants at exorbitant prices. Enraged by their betrayal, the peasants responded with riot and uprising.

The army was forced to restore order to the countryside, a campaign which laid the seeds for future generations of anti-tsarist revolutionaries.

The Communist leaders who succeeded the Tsars after the 1917 revolution similarly turned to force to reshape Russia. Lenin, the first leader of this Bolshevik Party, dreamt of a new type of society, free from inequality, exploitation and corruption. He was to die in 1924, though, a lonely and disillusioned man. He had managed to topple the Tsars, but failed to realize his hopes. Instead, just to maintain Bolshevik rule in the face of both internal resistance and pressure from Europe and the USA, he presided over the creation of a secret police force far more effective than that of the Tsars and laid the foundations of a bureaucratic dictatorship far more savage and exploitative than that which the Bolsheviks had toppled. His successor, Stalin, was more interested in power than in creating a new society. By means of an astonishingly organized and brutal campaign of state violence, in which perhaps 10 million Soviet citizens were executed, locked up in labour camps or worked to death, he industrialized the USSR, and fashioned a war machine able to end Hitler's dreams of an Aryan empire in the East and to roll in due course all the way into Berlin. Peter the Great, Lenin and Stalin were all very different characters, yet they shared a preparedness to use force in refashioning Russian society that ensured their lasting impression in history. Their legacy may not have been precisely what they intended or expected, but no one can doubt their impact upon Russia. Gorbachev was in many ways closer to Alexander II in his reluctance to use force and his naive belief that a free population would willingly do what a coerced population had previously been forced to do.

Brezhnev's USSR

Between Stalin's death in 1953 and 1982, the USSR was ruled first by Nikita Khrushchev and then by Leonid Brezhnev. As people, they were very different. Khrushchev was a wily and arrogant peasant, who had risen as Stalin's right-hand man and yet is remembered above all for denouncing Stalin's methods in his 'Secret Speech' of 1956. Khrushchev's era was marked by a series of reforms, initiatives and innovations which generated much sound and fury, but proved of little lasting impact. Ultimately, he was a transitional figure, shaped by the Stalin era and yet unable – and, to give him his due, unwilling – to rule by Stalin's methods. What he failed to appreciate was the extent to which, after the Second World War, the Soviet elite was no longer prepared to be dominated by one man. His removal in 1964 by a bloodless political coup reflected both his failure to keep the elite happy and their coming of age as a dominant ruling class.

Lenin, Stalin and Khrushchev had all, in their ways, tried to change the Soviet Union. With Brezhnev, though, the emphasis shifted to *managing* it. Instead of the grand plans, upheavals and utopian dreams of his predecessors, he offered a period of calm and security, an era of unprecedented prosperity from which everyone would benefit. After 50 years of revolution, civil war, industrialization, war and hunger, the Soviet people were seemingly being offered the chance to sit back and enjoy the fruits of their labours. This was at the heart of Brezhnev's style of government and the reason both for the decay of the Soviet system and also why today many look back at his time as some 'golden era'. Put crudely, the leadership bought everyone off, with benefits, perks and resources proportionate to their importance to the system. Ordinary Soviet citizens were offered a slowly but steadily improving standard of living. On a different scale, the same sort of deal was offered to the *apparatchiki*, the members of the Party elite. As individuals, as interest groups and as a class or caste as a whole, they were brought closer into the system, to ensure that all had a stake in keeping it running.

On paper, the Soviet system of government was a complex one, with three separate hierarchies (see Figure 1). According to the constitution (Stalin had revised it in 1936, and this version was merely tidied up by Brezhnev in 1977), the highest legislative body in the country was the Supreme Soviet. The word 'soviet' simply means 'council'. This parliament was made up of two chambers, each of 750 members. One, the Soviet of the Union, was directly elected from constituencies of around 300 000 voters; the other, the Soviet of Nationalities, was elected from each of the constituent republics and regions of the USSR. This sounds very similar to the US Congress, with its division between the House of Representatives and Senate, but the resemblance is only on the surface. In practice, the Supreme Soviet was a powerless sham. It was packed with Communist Party nominees, for a start: other parties were banned, and only one candidate stood in most elections. Voters – there either out of a sense of national duty, or because hard-to-find consumer goods were often available at polling stations – were expected simply to take their ballot paper and place it in the ballot box. If they wanted to cross out the Party's candidate or otherwise mark the paper, then they had to make obvious what they were doing, going into a polling booth to register a protest vote they knew would have no real effect on the overall election.

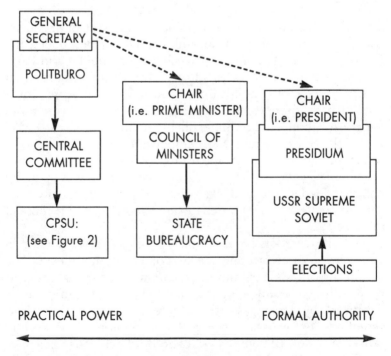

Figure 1: The Soviet System of Government Under Brezhnev

Not surprisingly, few chose this option. Why, after all, draw attention to yourself for the sake of a parliament which does next to nothing? The Supreme Soviet met only a couple of times a year for a few days to rubber-stamp the decisions made by the Presidium, its small (40-member) standing council. This Presidium had real power, not least over the budget, but its members were all senior Party members. As for the President, elected by the Supreme Soviet, this title was largely ceremonial. In theory, the government – the civil service, armed forces and other elements of the state bureaucracy – was responsible to the Supreme Soviet, but all the senior figures were members of the Party and under Party discipline. Real power, then, was vested not in parliament, but in the CPSU, the Communist Party of the Soviet Union.

The Communist Party of the Soviet Union

The CPSU was the brain, heart, sinews and tissue of the Soviet system. It was the Party leadership which decided policy, the Party-dominated bureaucracy which implemented it and Party structures and members which kept the country together. It certainly was not a political party in a Western sense. For a start, it had no opposition. Indeed, its power was written into the constitution, Article Six explicitly giving it a 'leading role' within the Soviet system. More importantly, its role and power were built into the state apparatus, giving Party members a dominant say at every level, from local council politics up to the national leadership, and excluding or persecuting any who tried to create avenues for debate and agitation outside those of the CPSU.

The CPSU's roots lay in Lenin's Bolshevik Party, formed in 1902 as an underground, revolutionary group seeking the overthrow of the Tsars and the creation of a Marxist order. It went through many changes since then, but can best be described by looking at five key events which shaped its evolution: its formation, the civil war, Stalinism, the Second World War and Brezhnev's era. The Bolshevik Party began as an illegal political movement and was thus organized for security and conspiracy. Lenin was an undoubtedly brilliant man, but also an arrogant and irascible one. While he valued debate, ultimately he impressed upon the Party a belief that success would only come through total discipline and central control. In this he was right, and it was the Bolsheviks' effectiveness and cohesion which ensured that they emerged the victors from the collapse of tsarist Russia in 1917. For all this, though, the Party retained a tendency towards a form of internal democracy and a proud idealism, that saw itself as a force using ignoble methods to reach a noble goal.

The anti-democratic side of the Party was strengthened, though, by the civil war which raged between 1918 and 1921. The Bolsheviks had to struggle to retain and extend their control over the country against a miscellaneous array of monarchists, anarchists, would-be military dictators, democrats, rival revolutionaries and foreign forces (including British, French, Japanese and US troops). A gritty and hard-fought battle for survival left no time for debate or idealism, and so many of the radical and democratic dreams of the Bolsheviks remained unfulfilled. The 'Old Bolsheviks', generally educated and cosmopolitan intellectuals, were swamped by a tide of 'New Bolsheviks' who joined what they saw as the winning side: in May 1917, the Party numbered around 80 000 members; by August this had risen to 200 000; following the revolution, this peaked at around a quarter of a million in March 1919. While many were genuine in their commitment, too often this was a commitment to the militarized Bolshevik Party of 1917, and not the original ideals of the Marxists. In other words, they were supporters of the ignoble methods more than the noble goal.

It was these 'New Bolsheviks' who were to be the basis for Stalin's rise to power after Lenin's death. He was in so many ways their ideal: more shrewd and crafty than intelligent, a user of people, utterly ruthless, anti-Semitic, nationalistic, ambitious. Old Bolshevik heroes such as Trotsky – brilliant, cocky, Jewish – and Bukharin – bookish, well-meaning, loyal – were all too easily out-manoeuvred and physically wiped out. Trotsky was exiled and eventually died in Mexico at the hands of one of Stalin's agents. Bukharin was shot as a traitor. In the

Great Purge of 1937–8, whole local leaderships were arrested and the officer corps decapitated (two-thirds of the army's marshals, corps and division commanders were arrested). Stalin believed above all in power, and having used the Party to achieve it, set out to ensure that those same people could not take it away. His main weapon was the secret police, which year after year purged the Party and the country, arresting, imprisoning or killing any real or potential threats to Stalin's power. He instilled a new culture within the Party, one made equally of fear, suspicion and ambition. After all, for every victim sent to the Gulag prison camps, someone else was promoted to take his place. This was a time in which people could rise very far, very fast within the Soviet system, so long as they could play by the rules of the game. There was little room for morality, for scruples, for any deviation from the official Party line coming from Moscow. The Party under Stalin was destroyed as a creative force, and instead became more an army of ambitious careerists, all working hard, echoing the official propaganda, with one eye looking for a chance to claw down their superiors and with the other keeping tabs on their own hungry subordinates.

This sort of piranha mentality could not last for long, though. It was too destructive, inefficient and exhausting. Ironically enough, it was the Second World War – the 'Great Patriotic War' to the Soviets – which brought about the next stage in the evolution of the Party. The Nazis threatened not only the Party's rule, but the physical extermination or subordination of the entire Slav people and an end to the very existence of the Russian state. In the face of such a threat, the country pulled together, and Stalin was forced to change his methods. Whereas once the able but unorthodox would have been replaced with mediocre but loyal Party hacks, the Motherland needed able leaders rather than yes-men. General Rokossovski, for example, was released from a Gulag and sent to command a mechanized corps. The Churches were reopened, as Stalin ditched Marxist rectitude for an appeal to older, Russian nationalist traditions. The war cost the USSR perhaps 28 million lives, yet the Union held together. From this conflagration emerged a very different Party. For one thing, it had acquired if not necessarily mass popularity, at least public legit-imacy. It had been the CPSU which had held the country together and led it to victory, and thus it gained the credit.

Until his death in 1953, Stalin was to seek in vain to regain the power over the Party he had had in the 1930s. Now more self-confident, held together by friendships forged in war and thus less open to Stalin's divide-and-rule tactics, the elite watched the balance of power swing to them, away from Stalin. While still the undisputed *vozhd* ('boss'), he was no longer the puppeteer pulling everyone's strings. On his death, he was planning a new round of purges once again to impose his will upon the elite, but this was not to be. In many ways, the Party changed little between 1953 and 1983. The beneficiaries of the purges of the 1930s and the Great Patriotic War, they now had everything to lose and little to gain from further chaos and upheaval. Instead, they tried to protect their comfortable status quo. They chose Khrushchev as their leader after Stalin because he promised just that. When he failed to deliver, when he not only tried to claw back Stalin's old dominance over the Party elite but also seemed to pose a very real danger to their power, they toppled him. Brezhnev proved much more willing and able to govern the country in the elite's interests.

The CPSU of Brezhnev's era was thus a strange beast. It had over 19 million full and candidate members (just under 10 per cent of the adult population), in every factory, submarine crew, school and collective farm. It had its own national daily newspaper (*Pravda* – 'Truth'), its own publishing houses, its own health farms, its own shops, its own telephone system. Essentially, it owned the USSR. In part, this was a class, the Soviet ruling class. Yet the Party contained ordinary shop-floor workers and farmhands as well as generals, professors and full-time politicians. It is perhaps more accurate to say that there were two parties. More than two-thirds of CPSU members were rank-and-file Communists, who may have joined out of genuine belief or more likely because of the perks which went with the Party card or because it was necessary for their career. Enrolling for a degree was difficult without evidence of Marxist–Leninist zeal, for example, while very few army officers ever made it beyond junior ranks without being members. Yet for most of these people, membership of the Party was no great affair. It meant attending tedious meetings, being roped in every so often for some propaganda campaign or the like. But a Party card could get you into special shops or ease some especially problematic loop of red tape. At this level, Party membership was perhaps most like membership of some moderately exclusive club.

The remaining third, though, were the Party activists who chose to become involved more closely and the *apparatchiki*, the CPSU's own full-time bureaucrats and managers. These are the true 'Party members' in the sense of the Soviet elite. Viewed very harshly, it could be said that the Party of the professors and politicians ran the prison; the workers' Party was for the trustees; and everyone else was just a common inmate. This is unfair, but it does at least convey some sense of the distinctions. Their diligence and efficiency, as well as their ability to play Party politics, could set them off on a career which would see them scaling up the Party's pyramidal structure to the very heights. These Party members were disproportionately drawn from the Slavic populations (Russians, Ukrainians, Belorussians), from men, from those with higher educations, from white collar professions. Above all, these were the people who involved themselves in the complex games of patronage and clientelism at the heart of Soviet politics. As usual, on paper the CPSU was a very democratic organization, with the basic Primary Party Organizations (which would group together all the members in, say, one factory or one farm) electing members of the regional councils and so on up the pyramid to the Politburo – effectively, the Party's 'cabinet' – which selected the General Secretary. In practice, power flowed up and down the system in small eddies of support and alliance. People low down the system looked to attach themselves and support rising stars who could drag them up in turn, just as those higher up sought to build themselves networks of allies and dependants below them, on whose support they could rely (see Figure 2).

(Mis)governing the USSR

Party politics could be an astonishingly complex game of alliance and patronage, but was vital to most successful careers because of the *nomenklatura* system. At its simplest, this was two lists: one of jobs, one of names. The first listed those jobs regarded as important to the state and Party, whether it be the director of Omsk's largest factory or the chief architect of Tomsk city council. The second list was of those people the local and central Party hierarchy deemed reliable, able and loyal enough for those important jobs. The logic is clear: to rise far in most careers you needed to have support from within the

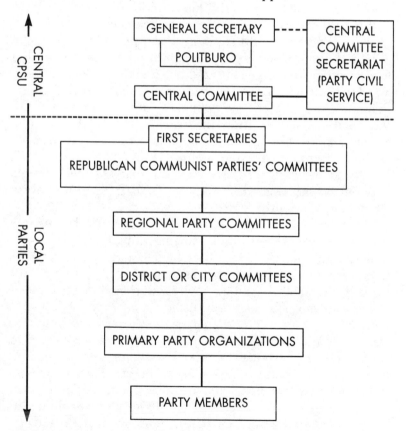

Figure 2: The Communist Party of the Soviet Union

CPSU, if not actually be a member. In this way, the Party also represented the USSR's ruling class, in that it brought together almost all the movers and shakers of the system – from generals to newspaper editors, industrial managers to film stars – and imposed some sort of common rules and identity upon them.

What in the West are the separate worlds of politics, business and bureaucracy were thus all embraced by the Party. This was most evident at the very top of the system, the Central Committee and Politburo. The Central Committee was a council of the 400–500 key members of the Soviet elite from across the country, representing its key sectors: the military, the civil service, the KGB, arts, science, the press, regional Party leaders. Officially, it was the heart and brain of the CPSU, electing the Politburo, controlling the Secretariat – the Party's own bureaucracy – and deciding Party policy. Given that it only met about twice a year, though, it was really above all a forum within which the elite could discuss the issues of the day and for the true masters of the country, the members of the Politburo, to sound out the opinions of their constituency. On the Politburo sat the most powerful leaders of the country, either as full (voting) or candidate (non-voting) members, such as the Foreign, Defence and Interior Ministers, the head of the KGB and the regional Party First Secretary of the Ukraine. Chaired by the General Secretary of the Party, it met every Thursday and ran the USSR.

Democratic systems, for all their flaws, do embody a variety of internal control measures, ranging from a free press and judiciary to equality before the law. Ultimately, governments must also face their electorates and be called to account through the ballot box. The Soviet system had none of these. Lenin had scorned such 'bourgeois' democracy for 'socialist democracy', which he had envisaged as being exercised by a strong, proud and vigilant working class through the local soviets. He ensured that this would not come to pass, though, by his reliance upon emergency measures and Party discipline. Before his death, he had come to realize the danger in this and was warning of the dangers of the Party-state becoming an unaccountable bureaucratic police state. Stalin destroyed the last traces of democracy, but his use of terror acted in some ways as a substitute, regularly clearing out the dead wood, keeping everyone on their toes. Since Stalin, though, the *nomenklatura* elite became increasingly secure. One of Brezhnev's slogans was 'trust in the cadres' – in other words, a promise that the state would not look too closely at what the elite were up to, so long as their activities did not threaten the state. In 1965, the Party-State Control Committee, one of the few remaining channels for popular control over the *apparatchiki*, was abolished. Even the KGB lost much of its ability to police the Party elite, concentrating instead on controlling the masses.

With the population bought off or controlled, the press and the police in its grip and free from the threat of a new Stalin, the Party became increasingly lazy and inefficient. It lost the sense of mission which had given it coherence in earlier days, and simply became a cosy and privileged caste. It even became ever more hereditary, as *apparatchiki* pulled strings to ensure their children received the education and jobs they needed to remain within this privileged world. It thus also became prey to massive and institutionalized corruption. To an extent, this is deeply rooted in Russian culture. Tsarist civil servants were expected to survive not on their salaries, but by *kormleniye* ('feeding'), accepting bribes and running private deals of their own. Under Brezhnev, though, corruption became endemic to the Party or state bureaucracy. On one level, this could be seen simply as part of the perks of the job, along with the car, driver and summer house. Soon, however, it began to eat into the legitimacy, efficiency and budget of the state. In Uzbekistan, for instance, almost the entire republican Party leadership was involved in a huge fraud which, between 1976 and 1983, embezzled the equivalent of $2 billion from the central government in return for millions of tons of non-existent cotton. Not only was the fraud masterminded by the then-Uzbek Party leader, Sharaf Rashidov, it even involved Brezhnev's son-in-law (then First Deputy Interior Minister).

This is important, because it was the Party that chose Gorbachev as its leader in March 1985, just as the abortive coup of August 1991 which finally laid him low originated from within the elite of the CPSU. Forged in conspiracy and war, it was by instinct secretive, hierarchical and suspicious of any challenges to its domination of the USSR. The personal politics of faction and alliance counted as much as ability or policies. Since Stalin, though, the governance of the country had moved away from the dictatorship of one man to a stifling, bureaucratic oligarchy. The Party brought together the country's elite, had its own civil service to shadow the 'official' civil service and permeated every aspect of Soviet government and society. It was above the law. It perpetuated itself, thanks to the *nomenklatura* system, which made a mockery of any pretence of democracy or accountability (or rather made people accountable only to the CPSU). Gorbachev's grandeur was that he was able to break the conditioning of 60 years of Party rule and try to change his country without violence and without the CPSU; his tragedy was that he was to fail.

Life, Soviet-style

Little proves the limited strengths and glaring weaknesses of Brezhnev's system so well as its management of the economy and thus the quality of life of the Soviet population. This, after all, is what politics is about. When the USSR fell, it did so ultimately because its leaders could not keep their promises to their people. They, hungry and angry, looked to new leaders, causes and ideologies in which to believe. As discussed above, for the ordinary citizens of the USSR, the Brezhnev era meant the so-called 'Little Deal'. In return for their willingness to sit back and let the Party run the country, they were offered freedoms and a standard of living which, while not up to Western standards, were unparalleled in Russian history. To a people who could still remember the days of Stalin, when turning up late for work could mean three years' forced labour, the freedom to turn up to work drunk and yet still keep the job really meant something. Even if they could still not oppose the power of the Party, or openly criticize it, the KGB would generally limit itself to a stern warning, or get the troublemaker demoted or sent to prison for a year; a far cry from the bullet in the back of the neck or the Siberian labour camps of Stalin's day.

Above all, this was a time of consumerism for most Soviet

citizens and of lax discipline; as the Russian saying went, 'they pretend to pay us, and we pretend to work'. The black market grew dramatically until it was almost impossible *not* to have to use it to gain hard-to-find foods, consumer goods or even medicines. Whereas the ruble became increasingly worthless, *blat* – the Russian word for 'pull', or 'connections' – became the most vital resource of all. In its own way, though, the 'Little Deal' worked. Tired of a half-century of drama, Soviet citizens were prepared to be bought off and leave running the country to the Party so long as it delivered on its promises of peace and plenty. The problem was that from the middle of the 1970s, the leadership was increasingly unable to keep this promise as a result of sharp economic decline. In 1978, Soviet economic growth effectively ended. By a vicious stroke of bad luck, that year also saw the first of a series of bad harvests. By 1980, bread was effectively having to be rationed in many areas.

The reasons for economic decline are several: natural backwardness, military spending, economic planning, bad luck and the consensual nature of Brezhnev's rule. First of all, it must be recognized just to what extent the USSR (like tsarist Russia) had always been a backward nation. Through the concentration of national efforts into very specific targets, Stalin had managed to create a war-fighting economy able to match that of Nazi Germany. This was, however, a very undynamic and unbalanced economy. It was able – thanks to the efforts of Soviet spies – to build its own atomic bomb in 1949 and launch a crude satellite into orbit ahead of the USA in 1957. Yet at the same time, many factories were still running machines in the 1980s built under Stalin or looted from Germany after the Second World War. At best, the Soviets were 6–10 years behind the West. By 1975, the USSR's Gross National Product (GNP – the best general gauge of national economic power) was still only 58 per cent of the USA's. GNP per capita (which reflects national economic efficiency) was less than 48 per cent of the USA's.

The USSR was a world superpower largely by virtue of its military strength, but this itself was a tremendous drain on these relatively scarce national resources. Military spending accounted for some 15 per cent of GNP. What is more, the defence industries managed to become fairly efficient only by becoming parasites. They developed at the expense of the rest of the economy, skimming off the best materials, hiring the brightest scientists, demanding priority access to new technology.

The whole Soviet approach to economic planning was itself a product of the Stalin era. The State Planning Committee, *Gosplan*, was established to manage the Soviet economy with the hope that this would allow maximum efficiency and productivity. Economies, though, are complex and dynamic systems beyond the capabilities of any committee. Under Stalin, the planned economy worked because it had very simple targets (the creation of a military industrial base) and, above all, because it was backed by terror. Factory managers who failed to meet their production quotas, farmers unprepared to hand over their crops to the state, workers who turned up late, all these could face terrible punishments meant, above all, to set a stern example to everyone else. In its own brutal and inefficient way, it did work. Yet Stalin's successors tried to use much the same system both with far more complex ends in mind and without the same use of coercion. This did not work. Instead, the USSR saw a steady decline in efficiency and productivity and the equally steady growth of a huge bureaucracy with little to do other than shuffle meaningless paper. By the end of Brezhnev's rule, there were around 14 million state civil servants, and another 11 million involved in administration within the economy – bureaucrats made up almost 30 per cent of the entire workforce.

For a while, though, the USSR was able to make up for the systemic shortfalls of its economy with windfall profits from good luck. US defeat in Vietnam, for example, helped create a climate conducive to Brezhnev's policy of *détente* in the late 1960s and early 1970s, a general easing of East–West tensions. From the Soviets' point of view, what made this important were the new opportunities to acquire Western markets and technology. The Arab–Israeli conflicts of the 1970s and the ensuing OPEC oil boycott drove up prices at a time when the USSR was the world's leading oil exporter. All the USSR's natural resources – oil, diamonds, natural gas – were plundered to provide the money to try and keep the system going.

That these were the lengths to which the leadership would go in order to avoid having to implement change underlines the extent to which political decay also played its part in economic decline. *Gosplan*'s economic models were based upon data which were often inaccurate or deliberately misleading, given the extent to which this was a time of widespread corruption and embezzlement. Perhaps more important were the consequences of the way policy-making within the inner elite of the Central Committee and Politburo had become dominated by consensus and compromise. Brezhnev had been eager to reassure his colleagues that he did not have the dictatorial tendencies of a Khrushchev or a Stalin. More to the point, his colleagues ensured that he could not establish the same sort of personal tyranny by limiting the powers of the General Secretary, in particular over appointment. By necessity and also by temperament, Brezhnev made the General Secretary's job into one of chairing rather than leading. His role was to broker deals within the elite, and bring everyone round to compromise decisions which left no one excluded. If with Stalin the General Secretary had been the undisputed Tsar of the USSR, Brezhnev was the cosy, comfortable mediator.

This style of leadership does have advantages. It meant an end to the erratic style of policy-making Khrushchev had exemplified, with policy being made almost on the spur of the moment. That had brought the Soviet Union to the brink of nuclear war with the United States over the Cuban Missile Crisis in 1962 and had led to the disastrous maize campaign when Khrushchev, impressed by a visit to Iowa in 1959, decreed the planting of maize all over the USSR, largely in areas wholly unsuited to the crop. On the other hand, it meant that all decisions were compromises hammered out by the key interest groups running the Soviet system. When the time came for tough decisions – as it did in the latter half of the 1970s – then this was a system with a built-in bias away from radical measures and within which any of these interest groups had, in effect, a veto. This was a time which called for a decisive and hard-headed leader to force change on the system, or a flexible and sophisticated elite prepared to sacrifice some of their power and privileges today to ensure that their rule had a tomorrow. Brezhnev was locked into his old role as mediator, though, and after his first stroke in 1976 became increasingly frail. It was to take reversals on the world stage to shock the elite into concessions.

Reading and Sources

This chapter seeks to set the Gorbachev era in its wider historical context and establish the contours of the system within which he had to operate. Quite which books should be awarded the crowns of the best general overviews of the Soviet regimes of 1917–82 is a difficult and very personal choice. I would direct readers towards Robert Service's magisterial *Lenin: A Political Life* (3 vols. 1985, 1991, 1995, Macmillan), Chris Ward's *Stalin's Russia* (1993, Edward Arnold) and William Tompson's *Khrushchev: A Political Life* (1995, Macmillan). Brezhnev's life has defied good biography, but many general studies of the 1970s and early 1980s provide the outline of his era and its problems. Of general surveys of the USSR, Geoffrey Hosking's *A History of the Soviet Union* (1990, Fontana), Martin McCauley's *The Soviet Union since 1917* (1993, Longman) and Mary McAuley's rather briefer *Soviet Politics, 1917–1991* (1992, Oxford University Press) have much to recommend them. As regards studies of particular issues, the last (third) edition of Ronald Hill and Peter Frank's *The Soviet Communist Party* (1986, Allen & Unwin) is still the best primer on this arcane institution, while Mikhail Voslensky's semi-autobiographical *Nomenklatura* (1984, Bodley Head) helps put the structures into a human context. In many ways, though, Arkady Vaksberg's *The Soviet Mafia* and Konstantin Simis's *USSR: Secrets of a Corrupt Society* (1982, Dent) really paint the starkest picture of the Brezhnevian elite at work and play.

2

YURI ANDROPOV AND THE RISE OF MIKHAIL GORBACHEV

By 1979, even the most complacent members of the Soviet leadership had begun to awaken to the problems facing their regime. To a large extent this was an internal problem, yet it took events outside the USSR's borders to bring home the scale of the danger facing them; specifically, events in Afghanistan and Poland. Afghanistan alerted the Kremlin to the threat posed by nationalism, in the non-Russian regions of the USSR in particular, while Poland raised the spectre of mass, working-class protest against hardships and mismanagement.

The pro-Soviet People's Democratic Party of Afghanistan (PDPA) had seized power in a coup in 1978. It soon became something of an embarrassment to Moscow. Although the Soviets could hardly disavow a fellow 'progressive' regime, they felt that the PDPA was not only hopelessly divided but also politically unsophisticated. The PDPA's leaders were almost Stalinist in their eagerness to turn a backward, agrarian nation into a modern industrial state along Soviet lines. Yet they did not realize how much weaker their forces were than Stalin's and the extent to which Afghanistan's tribes and clans – fiercely independent, passionate in their defence of Islam against the 'godless' Communists – would fight any 'revolution from above'. By October 1978, the majority of the country was in rebellion, the government's authority limited to the main towns. In March 1979, even the city of Herat rose in bloody rebellion, suggesting that the PDPA was also losing those remaining strongholds. The Soviets tried to persuade the regime to adopt a less confrontational line. Hopes for a more moderate line were dashed in September, though, when Afghanistan's Prime Minister Amin assassinated his more moderate partner in rule, Taraki. Amin repeatedly begged Moscow to send military aid, but when the Soviets did intervene they did so to replace him with a more tractable leader, Babrak Karmal. On 27 December 1979, Soviet paratroopers and special forces seized the capital, Kabul, and killed Amin, while four divisions of troops rolled across the Soviet–Afghan border.

This was to be the start of a brutal 10-year war of occupation, one which ultimately the USSR neither won nor lost, yet decided no longer to fight. The Soviet leadership had not expected such a prolonged operation. Although the KGB and the army had both warned of the risks of being bogged down, Brezhnev and Defence Minister Ustinov, in particular, thought that all it would take would be a brief show of force and the removal of the intransigent Amin. Above all, they felt that they could not afford not to intervene. Had the PDPA regime fallen, Moscow feared this would send dangerous signals across the world. Other Soviet client states in the Developing World would come to question just how valuable a patron Moscow really was, if it could not even protect an ally on its own borders. The USSR would also have lost face before the West. The United States, still smarting from its failure to rescue embassy staff held hostage by the new Islamic revolutionary government in Iran, could take great comfort from it. More importantly, in the light of the Iranian revolution of 1978–9, and a general fear that Islam in the Middle East was again on the rise, Moscow feared that a victory by Islamic fundamentalists over a Communist government would affect its own Central Asians. The population of the USSR contained a large and growing Central Asian population – 12 per cent of the total, but expected to reach 25 per cent by the year 2000 – which Moscow feared could be united against the Soviet regime by Islam.

As for Poland, in the 1970s the government had adopted a kind of 'Little Deal' there, too. The first half of the decade saw relatively strong economic growth, yet based largely upon running up a huge national debt. From 1975 or so, though, the government could no longer afford this policy, just at the time when the population had become used to improved standards of living. Poland's hard currency debt more than trebled between 1975 and 1980. The result was rapid economic slowdown and tumbling living standards. This, in turn, bred industrial action. In 1980, strikes in the factory city of Lublin spread across the country. Purely economic demands gave way to political ones, and local strike committees increasingly banded together under the banner of the Solidarity trade union. The Polish government tried to appease the strikers with concessions, yet without success. Moscow feared not only that Poland was falling out of her control, but that this unrest could spread. While the Polish government opened talks with the strikers, Warsaw Pact forces held manoeuvres on her border and East German and Czech reservists were called back to service. The Polish regime staggered on until December 1981, when Polish President General Jaruzelski declared martial law. A complex figure, Jaruzelski was looking for some way of pacifying both the Soviets and the strikers while holding the country together. His new policies combined firm action against political protests with economic liberalization and marketization. In a way, he succeeded, in that the country was subdued, Moscow mollified and, ironically, the groundwork laid for Poland's entry into the capitalist world in 1989. From Moscow's point of view, though, there was little comfort to be found.

What made events in Poland so worrying to the Soviet elite were the parallels which could be drawn with the USSR. There, too, economic crisis had, in effect, led to a repudiation of the 'Little Deal'. Standards of living were no longer rising in line with rising public expectations. This concentrated resentment at the privileged lifestyle of the *nomenklatura* elite. Beyond protests in the southern republic of Georgia in 1977, which had to be put down by force, and which were anyway triggered above all by the fear that the Georgian language itself was going to be outlawed, there were few overt signs of this resentment. Yet the evidence of rising social and political pressures were plain to see to those members of the elite with access to relatively authentic information. Despite the best efforts of the KGB, the dissident movement, largely drawn from the country's intellectuals, continued to survive. There were even attempts to form anti-government trades unions. In Poland, it was an alliance between unionized workers and liberal intellectuals which had made Solidarity so formidable, after all.

Medieval legend linked the health of the nation with that of the king, and the parallels between the state of the General Secretary and that of the USSR were striking. As Brezhnev slid further into moribund senility, the idealism of the revolution, the triumphant nationalism of Stalin, even the easy complacency of the early Brezhnev era, all gave way to a new feeling of unease within the Soviet elite. In 1980, the jamming of Western radio broadcasts to the USSR resumed, while a second poor harvest meant a return to bread rationing, for the first time since the Second World War. On the one hand, the elite was reluctant to take risks or try anything new. This was, as much as anything else, a result of its age: by 1981, the average age of the Politburo was 68. Yet on the other there was also a growing acceptance that something had to be done. But what, and by whom?

Yuri Andropov

The first to accept this daunting challenge was Yuri Vladimorovich Andropov. A man who in his time had been a Young Communist League organizer, a diplomat and then, for 15 years, the head of the KGB, he was a distinctive and powerful combination of reformer and conservative. It is this background that helps explain Yuri Andropov and why and how he laid the foundations for Gorbachev's revolution. Born in the south of Russia in 1914, his childhood years were full of war, revolution and civil war, while his politically formative years were to be dominated by the looming shadow of Stalin. As a young factory worker, he joined the Young Communists (*Komsomol*) at the age of 17, at a time when Stalin had just defeated his rivals for control of the Party and was embarking on his brutal programme of forced industrialization and agrarian reform. In 1936, he became a full-time *Komsomol* officer. Stalin's regular purges of the Party meant that anyone who showed the necessary combination of ability and political instinct could rise quickly, and Andropov was no exception. In 1940, he was made *Komsomol* First Secretary of the new Karelo-Finnish Republic. This was a very sensitive post for a 26-year-old to be holding, for the region had that year been conquered from Finland, and Andropov's task was to pacify and 'sovietize' it. In other such cases, Soviet officials simply relied on brutality and secret police tactics. It is striking that even at this early stage, while not shrinking from using the iron fist, Andropov showed a willingness to try and win active support rather than sullen submission. This trait would be especially visible later during his time in Hungary. During the Second World War, Karelia was occupied by German and Finnish troops, and Andropov co-ordinated partisan operations against them. After the war, he moved from the *Komsomol* to the main Party, and in 1951 he was transferred to Moscow to work within the Party's own civil service, the Central Committee Secretariat.

Shortly afterwards, though, he was sent to Hungary, first as Counsellor and then from 1954 as the Ambassador. Again, he was sent to a recently conquered region to help supervise its incorporation into the USSR's European 'empire', but again he managed to avoid falling into the arrogant and insensitive ways of so many of his counterparts. Almost uniquely for a Soviet ambassador, he even learnt the local language. In 1956, Khrushchev's tentative moves to roll back some of Stalin's excesses in Moscow led to a split within the Hungarian Party and an anti-Communist uprising. The Soviets responded with a massive military intervention which involved 200 000 troops, smashing the uprising at the cost of perhaps 25 000 Hungarian and 7000 Soviet lives. Andropov worked closely with the Soviet military command and secret police, yet proved to be a moderating influence. Even when, in 1957, he left Hungary, he was able to have an important role in developing its future relationship with the USSR since he was promoted to head the Central Committee's Socialist Nations Department. In the 10 years he ran it, Andropov turned a small, young department into an important fiefdom within the Soviet bureaucracy, with interests across the globe and a staff which included many of the best and the brightest of the academic elite.

The way Andropov developed Soviet–Hungarian relations after 1956 indicated his way of working. Broadly speaking, he applied three basic rules:

- Open resistance must be crushed as quickly and completely as possible. He had, for example, no qualms about the invasion and subsequent round-up of ringleaders.
- Suppression is far less effective than deterrence and, above all, co-optation. The very scale of the 1956 crack-down was used to try and cow any future resistance. More to the point, rather than trying to rule through a handful of loyal quislings, efforts were made to entice more respected individuals – the sort of people who might otherwise be threats to it – to join the regime.
- There is no point in trying to prevent *any* change or believing merely what one would *want* to believe. Although one of his long-standing rivals, Mikhail Suslov, tried to make Hungary little more than a puppet state, Andropov success-fully campaigned for the new regime to be allowed the freedom and flexibility to find its own way to develop, so long as it accepted the USSR's overall claim to control over the region.

These were principles he would apply when he was transferred to head the KGB in 1967. The first Soviet political police chief since its founder, Felix Dzerzhinski, not to end his career with execution or disgrace, he changed the very nature of the force. He inherited a Stalin-era machine of torturers, executioners and informants, but by his departure in 1982 had turned it into a business-like and flexible modern political police service. While still wholeheartedly and ruthlessly committed to the preser-vation of the Soviet order, it had become far more sophisticated. Increasingly recruited from the best universities, it above all became a force modelled on Andropov's three basic principles.

Where necessary, it repressed and eliminated its rivals, though even here it used rather more finesse than before. Once dissidents might have been shot or forced into slave labour;

increasingly they were instead quietly locked up in psychiatric hospitals or even just thrown out of the country. From 1971, Jewish and German emigration became a mass process, used by the Soviets in part as a way of ejecting troublesome dissidents and even common criminals. Far more effort, though, was put into deterring open resistance or, better yet, identifying potential problems and dealing with them before they even manifested themselves. Above all, Andropov's KGB became a powerful tool for gathering, processing and analysing information. Information, after all, is one of the basic resources of the modern state. Whereas once they prepared flatteringly rosy-tinted pictures of the world, the KGB's analysts were now asked to provide a genuine and accurate one. This was still a very imperfect process, given that the KGB was almost as riddled with corruption, inefficiency and back-sliding as the rest of the Soviet bureaucracy. Yet it did mean that Andropov probably had a truer picture of the real state of the USSR than any of the other Soviet leaders.

The KGB versus Brezhnev

From the late 1970s, this renovated KGB would be the cutting edge of a campaign to win Andropov the General Secretaryship of the CPSU. Not only did he have his own ambitions on the post, Andropov was also coming to see the short-sighted and selfish corruption and indolence of Brezhnev and his circle of allies as threats to the very future of the Soviet state and all it should stand for. He thus began a political campaign built around using anti-corruption campaigns both to undermine the Brezhnev clique and establish his own credentials. In 1978, for example, the Deputy Minister for the Fishing Industry, Vladimir Rytov, was arrested for his part in a criminal ring which was hiding expensive caviar in tins marked herring, for sale on the black market at high prices. Given what has been said before about the extent to which corruption had spread amongst the elite during the Brezhnev era, this was a dramatic development. Some Party grandees had overstepped the mark in previous years and been forced (usually at

Andropov's urging) to retire. Georgian Party First Secretary Vasili Mzhavanadze, for example, had openly consorted with and protected a notorious black marketeer and his wife 'acquired' a stolen diamond ring which Interpol was hunting. Even he, though, was allowed to retire gracefully in 1972 and accept a hefty pension. Rytov, though, was publicly tried and then executed. What is more, the investigations did not simply use him as a scapegoat. They led to the enforced retirement of Fisheries Minister Ishkov and eventually the downfall of Sergei Medunov, Party Secretary of the Krasnodar region on the Black Sea coast and a close friend of Brezhnev's.

It was clear that this new anti-corruption campaign was not just another empty propaganda exercise. It began to establish Andropov's credentials as a genuine opponent of the moral laxity of the Brezhnev era and gave the KGB some popular legitimacy it had previously lacked. It also represented a useful way of silencing, frightening, undermining or eliminating Andropov's main political rivals, most of whom were close Brezhnev cronies and thus, by definition, those whose snouts were deepest in the trough. In perhaps the greatest irony, Brezhnev was forced in 1979 to give formal support for the very campaign which was undermining him, signing a Central Committee decree 'On Strengthening Law and Order'. By 1980, Andropov's investigators were moving closer still to Brezhnev, his family and his closest colleagues, and the next year another spate of corruption scandals broke. The involvement of Brezhnev's daughter, Galina, with a black-marketeer known as 'Boris the Gypsy' became common knowledge, while General Semen Tsvigun committed suicide. This last was especially important as Tsvigun had been close to Brezhnev and appointed as Andropov's deputy at the KGB precisely to keep an eye on him. Tsvigun was presented with evidence of his own corruption and offered the choice of suicide or a public trial. He chose the former, and in doing so signalled the end of the good old days, when Brezhnev's favour counted for more than Andropov's enmity.

Perhaps the only rival to Andropov who could not be lumped neatly into the 'Brezhnev clan' was Suslov, the Central Committee Secretary for Ideology and, as such, perhaps the second most important figure within the Party. Not only were they political opponents, Suslov and Andropov cordially disliked each other, something perhaps explained by their similarities as much as their differences. Like Andropov, Suslov was a lean and ascetic puritan, scornful of the heavy-drinking, back-slapping insiders of Brezhnev's circle. Unlike Andropov, though, Suslov was inflexible and conservative, suspicious of anything that smacked of novelty and change. In January 1982, though, Suslov died, and Brezhnev, perhaps hoping to buy off Andropov and sever his links with the KGB, proposed him for Suslov's old post.

It was to be Brezhnev's last miscalculation. Andropov gladly accepted the promotion, yet left a loyal retainer, Vitali Fedorchuk, in charge of the KGB. More to the point, he kept up his political campaign, using the opportunities his newly-raised profile offered to the full. After all, he knew that he could not simply rely upon undermining his rivals; he had to establish a positive platform to win support. He used his new post as Ideology Secretary to develop two linked themes: the need for increased discipline – something which applied to everyone from factory hands to *apparatchiki* – and the application of this extra energy to economic modernization. Most importantly, this won him the support of Defence Minister Ustinov. While Ustinov was a friend of Brezhnev's, he lacked the General Secretary's taste for the high life and approved of Andropov's hard-working style. In particular, though, he was acutely aware that the USA's lengthening technological lead risked making his armed forces obsolete, and was ready to back a candidate willing to tackle this problem. By contrast, Brezhnev's close friend and preferred successor, Konstantin Chernenko, offered no new ideas. He ended up trying to rely on spreading rumours that Andropov was part-Jewish. Brezhnev himself was too far gone to be much help to him. In September, he had even began to read the wrong text of his speech while on live television.

Andopov in Power

By the time Brezhnev died, in November 1982, Andropov had already all but won the campaign to succeed him. He had the support of Foreign Minister Gromyko and Ustinov, while Chernenko lacked anything like Andropov's breadth of experience and intellect. Within a day of the announcement of Brezhnev's death Andropov was elected General Secretary, 'unanimously' endorsed by the Central Committee. The irony was that although there were no credible candidates to stand against him, many within the elite were very wary of him and their support could not be counted on. Besides which, Andropov was ill. While neither he nor anyone else fully understood just how soon his kidneys would fail, he appreciated that time was not on his side. As a result, Andropov's leadership strategy was built upon two pillars. First of all, he sought to win the political initiative and convince both the uncertain political elite and the masses that some kind of reform was both inevitable and viable. Secondly, he looked to replace or bypass those hide-bound and hostile grandees who had so grudgingly elected him with a new generation of political leaders who could implement those reforms.

For an elite so long accustomed to the cosy inertia of Brezhnev to accept the need for reform represented a major achievement. Andropov cannot claim all the credit. Instead, his election reflected the slow intrusion of the real world into the elite's haven of privilege. The economy had stagnated, with growth rates falling to near zero. The results were increasingly evident both in a demoralised and disillusioned population and also in the implications for individual political lobbies. The armed forces saw their strategic parity with the USA, achieved at great cost in the early 1970s, under threat from new generation weapons systems which could conceivably render their tanks and nuclear missiles obsolete. The KGB and the Interior Ministry (MVD) began to fear rising popular unrest in response to the state's inability to maintain the old policies of 'bread and circuses' (or perhaps rather 'sausage and televisions') whereby it had bought them off in the past. Experts had been warning for years of the crises to come, in particular a group of academics who had been meeting in Novosibirsk regularly since 1979. Their so-called 'Novosibirsk Report', circulated in 1983, was to become one of the founding manifestos of Gorbachev's reforms.

What Andropov did was to take these individual and specific concerns and set them in an overall context. With events in Afghanistan and Poland still in their minds, the elite could come to realize that their very grip upon the USSR might be at risk. It was better, they conceded, to put up with Andropov's reforms and anti-corruption campaigns now than risk revolution or civil war tomorrow. At least, they appreciated that his time at the KGB meant that Andropov had the clearest picture of the real state of the nation and the best tools to do something about it. From the very beginning, Andropov sought to hammer home to the elite how dangerous was their position. With a candour totally out of keeping with the comforting old clichés of the previous order, he warned that many of the old ways 'have failed the test of time' and that the economy was being run in 'a quite irrational manner of trial and error.'

Quite what he would do, though, neither they nor Andropov himself really knew. Andropov – like Gorbachev after him – was to come to power knowing that there was a problem which needed to be addressed, but with little real notion of how. In his first major speech as General Secretary, in November, he warned that while he had no 'ready recipes' for change, 'you cannot get things moving by slogans alone.' Instead, he promised to concentrate upon finding ways 'to speed up work to improve the entire sphere of economic management.' After all, this was at the heart of Andropov's task. He did not want to shake up the existing political system and above all the position of the CPSU. Quite the opposite, he wanted to shore it up by revitalising the Soviet economy and weeding out those members whose obvious misuse of their positions were bringing the Party into disrepute.

To do this, though, he needed people who could come up with new ideas, who were prepared to implement them, who had largely avoided the Brezhnevite orgy of corruption and who could carry on his work during his months of illness and after his death. Here, too, Andropov used the November speech to signal his intentions. 'Perhaps', he speculated, 'some people simply do not know how to tackle the job [of reform].' For them, he concluded, 'it is necessary to think what kind of assistance must be given to these comrades.' At best, he was offering pensions. Andropov soon embarked on a purge of the more incompetent and corrupt upper elite and the wholesale introduction of relative youngsters and outsiders, an 'Andropov Team' to take on the legacies of Brezhnev's 'Dnepropetrovsk mafia'.

Railways Minister Pavlovski was sacked, then Interior Minister Shchelokov, who later committed suicide rather than face trial on corruption charges. Yuri Sokolov, the manager of the prestigious Gastronom Number One food store and a notorious black marketeer, was arrested. A whole slew of reshuffles and transfers led to a series of important promotions. Nikolai Ryzhkov, a former director of the huge *Uralmash* industrial complex, was brought onto the Secretariat, as was Yegor Ligachev, the former Party First Secretary of Tomsk in Central Siberia and a renowned enemy of corruption. Fedorchuk moved over to the Interior Ministry and another close ally of Andropov's, Viktor Chebrikov, took over the KGB. Lev Zaikov, a state bureaucrat recognised as an honest and efficient administrator took over as Party Secretary in Leningrad, the USSR's second city. Vitali Vorotnikov, the man who cleaned up Krasnodar region after the downfall of Sergei Medunov, moved on to become Premier of the Russian Republic. Geidar Aliyev, the First Secretary of Azerbaijan and a man with a reputation (albeit largely undeserved) as a tireless fighter against corruption, was promoted to full (voting) membership of the Politburo. Most important, though, was undoubtedly the rise of the Central Committee Secretary for Agriculture, Mikhail Gorbachev.

Mikhail Gorbachev, Heir Apparent

To some extent, Gorbachev's career to that point had been the model of the high-flying Party *apparatchik's*. Born and bred in the southern Russian region of Stavropol, he rose quickly within the system to become First Secretary of the region in 1970. In part this was through his own energy and ability, and in part it reflected his knack for cultivating useful patrons, including both Suslov and Andropov. Himself a native of Stavropol, Andropov met Gorbachev regularly during his holidays, and from their formal contacts grew a friendship and a political alliance. Andropov saw in the younger man an *apparatchik* who had managed to retain a basic honesty and a genuine commitment to Marxism-Leninism while rising within the system. He had even managed to avoid many of the temptations of office; whereas most Soviet politicians saw it as only right and proper that they enjoyed the perks of their office and bent the rules to look after their family and friends, the Gorbachevs lived in comparative austerity. In Stavropol he had successfully managed to balance local interests with the dictates of Moscow and in the process enriched and modernised the region. In short, Gorbachev had both a keen awareness of many of the problems and contradictions of the Soviet system and yet an unquestionable commitment to it.

The death in 1978 of Gorbachev's previous sponsor, Kulakov, left an opening in Moscow and Andropov made sure his new protégé would fill it. In September, he engineered a fateful meeting at the Mineralye Vody railway station in Stavropol region, which brought together the current and three future General Secretaries. Brezhnev and Chernenko stopped on their way to Azerbaijan and for two hours met with Gorbachev and Andropov, a chance for Gorbachev to impress and flatter his way to Moscow. Two months later he was summoned to take up the post of Central Committee Secretary for Agriculture. At the age of 47, he was by far the youngest of the Secretaries, but the precocious Gorbachev's career rise showed no signs of slowing.

The agriculture portfolio had always been an important but dangerous one. Soviet farming was in an appalling state, and the USSR even had to import grain from the USA. In many ways, the agriculture problem was a microcosm of the general Soviet economic malaise. Farmers had lost their own land in the 1930s and since then had been forced into collective and state farms as employees, with no real incentive to work hard or improve their productivity. It is striking just how effective they could be when they had a real stake in the proceeds: the private plots of land which represented no more than 3 per cent of the entire cultivated area accounted for almost a quarter of all fruit and vegetables produced. Not only were the farm workers alienated, they were having to cope with antiquated and rusting machinery for which there was no more money to buy replacements. What they did manage to produce was all too often stolen to sell on the black market or simply wasted as a result of bureaucratic confusion and inefficiency. A third of the potato crop and a fifth of the grain harvest were simply left to rot each year because there were just not the storage facilities, trains or lorries available at the right place at the right time.

Although the 1978 crop was good, the harvests of 1979 and 1980 were nothing short of disastrous. Grain yields dropped from 237 million tons in 1978 to 180 and then 158 million. By 1980, the USSR was spending $7.2 billion annually on food imports, and even then could not avert rationing. That agriculture was just a stepping stone for him and that Andropov was protecting him was clear in the way Gorbachev's career did not suffer as a result. As it was, there was very little Gorbachev could do: the problems facing agriculture were part of the overall economic crisis and could not be tackled with piecemeal individual measures. Brezhnev's 1982 Food Programme was just one such hotch-potch, and Gorbachev pointedly distanced himself from it, realizing full well it would be ineffective. Instead, he was at least able to begin to ask the right questions, especially on the whole issue of providing greater incentives for farmers to produce.

As soon as Andropov was in power, he turned to Gorbachev. First he broadened the younger man's portfolio to include a wider range of domestic issues and then he began involving him in foreign affairs. In February 1983, Andropov fell ill and began to undergo dialysis for his various kidney problems. It became clear that he was grooming Gorbachev as his successor, by slowly giving him the public profile and range of experiences necessary for a new General Secretary. In April, Gorbachev was granted the signal honour of giving the keynote address on the anniversary of Lenin's birth. Next month, he led a trip to Canada which consolidated his new reputation as a confident and able diplomat. Nevertheless, Gorbachev was relatively new to the Kremlin and time was running out. In September, Andropov's health worsened further and in October one of his kidneys had to be removed. From that point on, he never left his hospital room. His mind remained unimpaired, but with their master and patron bed-ridden and clearly soon to die, Gorbachev and the other members of the 'Andropov team' found themselves harder and harder pressed. The silent majority of essentially conservative Soviet leaders, with Chernenko at their head, regained heart and with it some of the political initiative. In particular, as discussed in the next chapter, they blocked attempts to make Gorbachev Andropov's direct successor.

Andropov's Death: the Last Hope of the CPSU?

When Andropov died in February 1984, so, probably, died any chances of the CPSU's long-term survival. While Gorbachev believed himself a loyal 'Andropovian', he was at once too much a politician and a sentimentalist to follow his mentor's path. Andropov's was the dispassionate ruthlessness of the surgeon, cutting away the diseased without a second thought, in order to save the healthy. It did not make him an unfeeling robot – far from it, private accounts testify to the almost shy geniality of a man who still wrote poetry to his wife while heading the KGB. Gorbachev, by contrast, was a man of the heart. His desperate efforts to reform the Party, his rambling and emotional speeches, his eager cultivation of Western public opinion, all reflected a man of boundless faith in himself, in his beliefs and in his role in history.

A Soviet political joke doing the rounds in 1984 asked: how old is the socialist system in Russia? Sixty-seven years? No, only seven: six years under Lenin and one after Andropov. There is more than a little truth in this. While by the time of his death Lenin had come to appreciate that the Soviet system was becoming dehumanized, bureaucratized and tyrannical, he was no democrat. Stalin, Khrushchev and Brezhnev all twisted his ideas in their own interests, where Andropov sought instead to cut away 50 years of distortion and return to the harsh and purposeful purity of the original Bolsheviks. Yet if historical parallels are to be drawn, then perhaps they should rather be with Tsars Nicholas I and Alexander II, in the mid-nineteenth century. Nicholas saw himself foremost as a soldier, an unwilling Tsar who saw in military discipline a chance to save and reform Russia. His traditional image has been of a militarist, a harsh and unbending tyrant, devoid of imagination. Of late, though, scholars have begun to redress the balance, uncovering a man who felt an outsider to the self-deluding pageantry of court, and who became desperate to overcome the corruption and inefficiency undermining the state. His successor, Alexander II, is hailed as the 'Tsar-Liberator' who freed the peasants from serfdom, but the emancipation plans were actually drawn up during his predecessor's reign, by a commission Nicholas personally established. What is more, it was Alexander's naive belief that the peasants would respond with hard-working devotion and his preparedness to compromise the essentials of his decree to keep the aristocracy happy which sabotaged the plans. One of the great 'what-ifs' remains: how emancipation would have worked out had Nicholas ever steeled himself to introduce it, given that Nicholas – unlike Alexander – was prepared to deal mercilessly with resistance, whether from the masses or the elite.

Andropov remains another 'what-if'. Almost before he had even moved into his new office, he was laid low by kidney problems. Already dying, his efforts would be occupied with safeguarding his political legacy in the form of the 'Andropov team' and dealing with the unexpected. He was, after all, unlucky. He had hoped to ease relations with the West, not least to make it easier for him to negotiate a withdrawal from Afghanistan and bilateral arms reductions, to lighten the defence burden on the Soviet budget. In September 1983, though, Korean Air Lines flight 007 wandered accidentally into Soviet airspace. Air defence commanders, convinced it was a US spy plane trying to monitor missile tests in the region, panicked and shot it down, killing all 269 on board. It was a tragedy more than an atrocity, precisely the sort of incident likely when nations fall prey to paranoia and the temptation to arm rather than talk. Nevertheless, it overshadowed and doomed any attempts either to encourage West European public opinion to resist the deployment of new US nuclear missiles on their soil or to engage in any fruitful negotiations with Washington.

Nevertheless, Andropov left Gorbachev an impressive legacy. He had taken the Soviet elite and from their confused concerns that something was going seriously wrong he fashioned a grudging consensus that reform was necessary. A shrewd judge of character with a talent for attracting to himself able and varied allies, he had assembled a powerful 'team' for Gorbachev to lead, from academics to *apparatchiki*, journalists to secret policemen. Without Andropov, it is likely that there would have been no Gorbachev era. Not only was it he who brought Gorbachev to Moscow, but without him to lay the groundwork for reform, Gorbachev's subsequent plea for renovation would have fallen on deaf ears. A former head of the KGB, Andropov could preach the need for change without anyone questioning his information or his commitment to the Soviet state. The scourge of corruption, Andropov could isolate and undermine his rivals without anyone daring to oppose him. A man whose breadth of experience and intellect set him apart from the rest of Brezhnev's court, Andropov could establish a whole new agenda for a political system dominated for almost 20 years by self-indulgent conservatism. Andropov was a reformist rather than a revolutionary, he wanted to modernize and cleanse the Soviet system rather than change it in its essentials, but for all that he was the godfather of the Gorbachev revolution.

Reading and Sources

Although several biographies were written during or shortly after his time in office, there is no good study of Andropov's life and reign written with the benefit of the *glasnost'* of the 1980s. Archie Brown's article 'Andropov: discipline *and* reform', in *Problems of Communism*, volume 32, number 1 (1983), remains an excellent and insightful analysis, while John Parker's *Kremlin in Transition, volume 1* (1991, Unwin Hyman) contains a detailed study of the domestic and, especially, foreign politics of the time. Martin Ebon's biography *The Andropov File* (1983, Sidgwick and Jackson) is analytically lightweight, but does have an appendix containing an extremely useful collection of his speeches. Zhores Medvedev's biography *Andropov* (1993,

Blackwell) is better. Boris Fedorov's article 'Khrushchev, Andropov, Brezhnev: the issue of political leadership', in *Perestroika Annual*, edited by Alexander Yakovlev (1988, Futura), is an interesting comparative study from a Soviet political scientist who worked with Andropov in his time. Amy Knight's *The KGB* provides the best insight into how Andropov ran the political police.

3

ELECTING GORBACHEV

On the surface, Andropov's death on 9 February 1984 was treated much like Brezhnev's. Soviet television played the same sober music, *Pravda* ran suitably deferential obituaries and his funeral was another piece of Party pageantry, from the goose-stepping honour guard to the mourners with their red armbands. Much had changed, though, in the past fifteen months. No one seriously could pretend there was no need for some sort of reform. The new leader, Konstantin Chernenko, was visibly sick. His breathing was difficult and he could not even read out the formal eulogy to Andropov without pausing for breath and losing his place in the script. In Muscovite circles, the assessment of the new General Secretary was '*on ne tot*', 'he is not the one'. There was a palpable sense that change was in the air, that the times would require a different leader and – judging from Chernenko's appearance – that they would need him sooner rather than later.

Andropov's Last Months

In many ways, December 1983 had seemed to be a high-point for the 'Andropov team'. Although Andropov himself was confined to hospital, in dialysis, there seemed hope that he could survive another few years: more than enough time to arrange an orderly transfer of power to his understudies. After a lull, the appointment of reformists to key post resumed. A colleague and client of Gorbachev's since 1978, Nikolai Kruchina, took over as Central Committee Administrator of Affairs, a powerfully broad position, while the announcement of new elections to the Supreme Soviet in March 1984 promised a fresh reshuffle.

Then, Andropov used the Central Committee plenum meeting of 26 December to reaffirm many of the underlying principles of his model of cautious reform:

- that both greater labour discipline and more sensible and flexible management was needed to drive economic reform;
- living standards and the quality of goods produced had to be improved;
- defence spending had to be limited (the defence budget was unchanged for the fourth successive year; in real terms, this was equivalent to a steady reduction);
- government expenditure should be gradually transferred from the traditional heavy industrial sectors to public services and light industry.

What is more, the plenum was yet another opportunity for the consolidation of the 'Andropovians'' grip on power. Russian Republic premier Vitali Vorotnikov was promoted from non-voting to full member of the Politburo while KGB Chair Viktor Chebrikov became a non-voting member, and Yegor Ligachev got his place in the Secretariat. Immediately after the plenum there was also an extensive purge of regional Party leaders. This was the largest reshuffle of senior figures since 1978 and not only reflected Andropov's authority but also Gorbachev's clever behind-the-scenes stage management of the plenum.

Beneath the surface, though, not everything was going Andropov's way. He might be General Secretary, but he was also a bed-ridden invalid, dependent upon his underlings and forced to work within a political system which since Stalin's days had developed precisely to stop a powerful *vozhd* ('boss') from imposing his will upon the Soviet elite. He had, for example, been unable to attend the December plenum and instead copies of his speech were distributed to everyone there. In his final draft, Andropov had included an unprecedented suggestion that in his absence, Gorbachev should stand in for him at key meetings. In effect, this would have made explicit Gorbachev's position as Andropov's deputy and heir. In the printed version, though, this passage had been cut.

For in January 1984 the see-saw of late Soviet politics was to tilt the other way. Those Brezhnevite stalwarts Prime Minister Tikhonov and Konstantin Chernenko seemed restored to prominence. Their names appeared at the head of the list of those signing an obituary in *Pravda* on 16 January – one of those bizarre but telling clues as to position within the Kremlin pecking-order. That same day, the newspaper ran an editorial pouring cold water on the START East–West nuclear arms talks. So what had happened? In part, this was as a result of Andropov's successes in December. Those outside Andropov's circle, who had hoped to ride out the reshuffles, became increasingly fearful for their futures and rallied round their only credible protector, Konstantin Chernenko. But the speed with which Chernenko was to succeed Andropov and the way in which he accepted Gorbachev as his deputy suggest something more, that a deal was struck.

This was, after all, the essence of late Soviet politics: deals being hammered out in secret between powerful grandees and interest groups, behind a facade of fraternal unity and Party discipline. Foreign Minister Gromyko and Defence Minister Ustinov proved once again to be the king-makers. They broadly supported Andropov's line of cautious reform to modernize the USSR. As long-serving political veterans (aged 74 and 75, respectively) they also understood the bitterness and dismay of the old elite in the face of the anti-corruption campaign and the sudden rise of a new generation of political figures. In particular, regional Party leaders resented the new line, in that it represented a betrayal of the *laissez-faire* attitudes of the Brezhnev era. Having become accustomed to free reign, they now found Moscow meddling in their power bases. Kazakh Party First Secretary Kunayev, for example, had been a close friend of both Brezhnev and Chernenko, and had showered them with gifts. The anti-corruption campaign had forced him to dismiss one-third of his local Party bosses, all political clients of his own. With the Politburo sharply divided, Gromyko and Ustinov brokered a deal between the two wings, whereby Chernenko would be recognized as Andropov's successor-in-waiting, but that Gorbachev would in turn become his deputy and heir. Chernenko would have to accept that while he could slow down the campaigns Andropov had set in motion, he could not stop or reverse them.

Gratefully seizing his last opportunity both to make his name and protect his friends, Chernenko agreed. Gorbachev and the other 'Andropovians' also had little alternative. They could not afford to alienate Gromyko and Ustinov. Gorbachev still lacked the experience and profile yet to make a convincing solo bid for the General Secretaryship. Better then to strike such a deal now than risk the job going to someone younger and stronger. Chernenko, after all, was 72 and suffering from an advanced case of the lung disease, emphysema. He had been sick for several months in 1983 and it was unlikely he would stand in the reformists' way for long. By the time the bands had finished playing out the third state funeral, Gorbachev should be ready for power.

The Chernenko Interregnum

The succession was thus again all but a foregone conclusion. After Andropov's death on 9 February, there was a hurried weekend of last-minute haggling, but on Monday 13 February 1984, the Central Committee was duly informed of the Politburo's recommendation of Chernenko's candidature, a recommendation it promptly rubber-stamped. From the first, though, it was clear that Chernenko's reign would be little more than a temporary interregnum. While Chernenko could barely suppress his glee at certain moments during Andropov's funeral, his ill-health was obvious. His inability even to hold a salute or deliver a speech without pausing for breath was broadcast live on television to the Soviet people and the world. The cameras also showed the new faces within the leadership whom Andropov had raised, a sober and purposeful phalanx behind the coffin of their dead patron. They lost no time in asserting their strength within the new order. Within a couple of days it was publicized that the closing address at the Central

Committee plenum which elected Chernenko had been made not, as was usual, by the new General Secretary, but by Gorbachev. What is more, his speech was pointedly a warning. He omitted any praise for the new leader and instead extolled the virtues of Andropov and his reforms. Chernenko was being reminded of the terms on which he was elected, a reminder which was to be repeated by other 'Andropovians' in the next few days and weeks. The editor of *Pravda* even publicly labelled Gorbachev as 'number Two in the Soviet Union'.

Chernenko's 13 months have been characterized as a time of drift or even chaos. This lack of evident unity and purpose largely reflect the extent to which different agendas, programmes and strategies were at work, sometimes in parallel, sometimes at cross-purposes, with Chernenko too weak politically and physically to impose any co-ordination. The main processes at work were three:

- Chernenko tried – in vain – to assert his own political authority. To a large extent, though, his political and physical weakness was such that he could do little but enact the most trivial and petty of changes.
- Individual political actors and institutions did their best to use the lack of clear leadership and the power struggle to advance their own causes.
- The reformers defended themselves from Chernenko's attacks, worked to increase their own power base, and above all developed Gorbachev's claim to the succession.

Chernenko tried to assert his own authority in several ways. In time-honoured Soviet style, attempts were made to create a 'cult of personality' around him. His career as a Border Guard in the 1930s was dredged up and mythologized; skirmishes with bandits became vital struggles against counter-revolution, while a letter in the army newspaper *Krasnaya zvezda* hailed him as a crack shot and master horseman. As wits soon remarked, though, it is hard to create a cult of personality in the absence of a personality. Chernenko's career as a Party fixer and Brezhnev's crony did not lend themselves well to purple prose. Above all, he needed some successes to mark his term of office. If nothing else, he realized he had little time in which to mark his place in history. He authorized the escalation of the running war in Afghanistan, involving major bombing raids and huge land offensives, making him the only General Secretary seriously to think about trying to win the war by purely military means. Having briefly flirted with the idea of arms cuts, he then seemed instead determined to burn every bridge left from the relaxation in international tensions in the 1970s or built by Andropov. After launching an over-blown propaganda campaign about US military intentions, he then took the widely derided decision to boycott the Los Angeles Olympics as a tit-for-tat response to the Western refusal to attend the 1980 Moscow Olympics following the invasion of Afghanistan. West Germany was publicly accused of 'revanchism', the usual Soviet code for Nazi tendencies. China, with whom Andropov had opened new contacts, was snubbed. At home, Chernenko shifted the focus of Andropov's discipline campaign back towards punishing dissidents and slack workers. Foreign pop music was banned for its 'subversive' and 'unhealthy' content. Yelena Bonner, the wife of the celebrated dissident Andrei Sakharov, was threatened with charges of treason and prevented from travelling abroad for heart treatment.

For some, this array of conservative and xenophobic policies even suggested a swing back towards Stalinism. Chernenko himself strengthened this impression when he suggested returning to the city of Volgograd its previous name, Stalingrad. It would, however, be going too far to represent these as aspects of any coherent policy. Chernenko was old, sick, weak and desperate. Many of these initiatives – most notably in Afghanistan – were simply short-termist and generally shortsighted attempts to achieve at least some success before surrendering to emphysema and that looming third official funeral. They also represented overtures to various key interest groups he needed in order to balance or overcome the reformers. The hard line on dissidents, for example, was in part motivated by the hope of wooing the KGB away from Gorbachev's camp, just as Chernenko's tough words on arms control talks were as much as anything else intended for the ears of his own generals. As will be discussed later, the fact was that as Chernenko was not prepared to pledge any more money to the military, words were about all he could offer. Yet more of Chernenko's triumphs were lies, or rather, expressions of an age-old Russian tradition: *pokazhuka*, 'window-dressing'. In September 1984, for example, great public festivals celebrated the completion of the BAM link, a second trans-Siberian railway meant both to guarantee the security of the USSR's Far Eastern flank and open up more resources for the economy. Years later, it emerged that the line had not really been completed and would not be until 1989. Millions of kilometres of track rusted and had to be replaced as a consequence of this pointless 'Potemkin railway'.

Gorbachev's Rise

In part, Chernenko's inability to carry through any coherent policies or groom a successor of his own reflected the strength of the 'Andropov team'. While to a large extent this does mean Gorbachev, it is worth dwelling briefly on the nature of the group around him. From Andropov he had inherited not so much a tight-knit band of followers so much as a broad coalition united only by its belief that some kind of reform was necessary. It included generals such as Deputy Chief of the General Staff Sergei Akhromeyev, who were worried about trying to defend the USSR with an army of disillusioned and unhealthy conscripts armed with out-of-date weapons. It included liberals such as Roy Medvedev who wanted to see the country reformed into a 'socialist democracy' and puritan Leninists such as Yegor Ligachev. It included cunning careerists such as the Azeri Party Secretary Geidar Aliyev who had simply concluded that this was the horse to back. This variety was in the end to lead to the collapse of the reformist coalition and thus the last, best hope to save the USSR, but that was only after Gorbachev actually had to turn his general slogans into concrete policies. For the moment, though, in variety there was strength. The coalition could appeal to every sector of the elite, and carry within itself a wide and exciting range of ideas and debates. At its heart was Gorbachev, a politician who matured quickly once out from under Andropov's shadow. He proved his ability as a mediator and political deal-maker. Thanks in part to these alliances, he was able to neutralize attempts to undermine his position as heir apparent. Indeed, he worked hard and well to establish his fitness for the job. His greatest abilities – and his real enthusiasm – were, after all, in the arts of politics rather than the detail of administration and policy.

He had had to develop those skills from the first. He was born in Stavropol in 1931, when Stalin's collectivization campaign was ravaging the rich rolling farmlands of the south. Stavropol region erupted into rebellion and was forcibly quelled. He joined the *Komsomol* in 1946 and in 1950 won a place to read law at Moscow State University (MGU). For a young combine harvester operator to make it to MGU, the prestigious training ground for the future Soviet elite, makes it clear that he had not just intelligence and ambition, but also political contacts. His hard work as both a labourer and as a Young Communist agitator had already earned him the Order of the Red Banner of Labour at the age of 19 and brought him to the attention of the local Party. He arrived at MGU during Stalin's last years, a time when the triumphalism that had followed victory in the Second World War was giving way to a new mood of suspicion and disquiet as the ageing Stalin slipped further into paranoia. Gorbachev joined the Party while studying and some suggest he informed on his fellow students to the secret police to win favour. This could have been true, but does not actually say that much about him: every student, especially at MGU, was expected to be a loyal Communist, and during the Stalin era that inevitably meant collaborating with the secret police. It may sound sordid, but it was the normal way of the times, especially for a provincial lad with none of the high-level contacts and protection of so many of his Moscow-born fellows. While at MGU he met, wooed and wed Raisa Titorenko, an extremely gifted student of philosophy and Marxism-Leninism. Following graduation, they returned to Stavropol where he began work as an *apparatchik*, a full-time political bureaucrat. There he rose steadily, first through the ranks of the *Komsomol* and then the Party, and by 1970 became Stavropol Party First Secretary at the early age of 39. So far, this is a typical trajectory, helped not only by Gorbachev's evident energy and ability but also the happy chance that made Stavropol a favoured holiday spot for the Soviet leadership. As a matter of protocol, Gorbachev met and welcomed them all and made far more contacts and friendships than a local Party secretary usually would. In particular, he won the patronage not just of his predecessor in charge of Stavropol, Felix Kulakov, but also both Suslov and Andropov. It was Suslov and Andropov who brought him to Moscow in 1978 to become Central Committee Secretary for Agriculture and then, in short succession, a non-voting 'candidate' member of the Politburo in 1979 and a full member the next year.

Even in his early career, though, there were signs that Gorbachev was more than just another bright young *apparatchik* on the make. In particular, he was clearly far more open to different ideas and cultures than was wise or usual in the Stalinist era. Gorbachev's paternal grandfather was reportedly deported to Siberia, but his maternal grandfather ran the local collective farm. This mixed heritage, part dissident, part loyal official, sums up much of his character. As a child, he had been baptized, and while never a believer, Gorbachev retained some respect for religion and the faith it could inspire. At university, he met and became friends with Zdenek Mlynar, a Czech Communist who went on in 1968 to be involved in the attempt to create 'socialism with a human face' in Czechoslovakia. Mlynar later recalled conversations in which Gorbachev openly questioned Stalin's collectivization, drawing on the experiences of Stavropol. He travelled abroad on official visits to West Germany, Italy, Belgium, France and Czechoslovakia. He would also acquire a first-hand knowledge of the capitalist world no Soviet leader since Lenin could match, when the Gorbachevs travelled independently in France and Italy in the 1960s. Finally, there is also his relationship with Raisa to consider. In such a chauvinist and sexist culture, for a powerful and prominent man to acknowledge his wife as an equal partner (and his intellectual superior) was unusual; for him to continue to do so when it became a political liability, as it did in the 1980s, was remarkable.

The 'Second General Secretary'

As Chernenko's deputy-come-rival, he realized he needed to show that he was more than a country boy made good. His foreign travels in particular proved more than merely ceremonial engagements, and even shed more light on Gorbachev's talents and his views. In December 1984, for example, he visited London in a trip which did much to establish both his credentials as a diplomatic operator and his profile in the West. In a finely judged performance, he showed both his smile and his much-vaunted 'teeth of iron'. Government and business figures alike were seduced by his ready mastery of the issues in discussion, his quick wit and his attentive charm, while an attempt by one questioner to raise the KGB's treatment of dissidents was met not by propaganda or anger but a quick riposte: 'I could quote you a few facts about human rights in the United Kingdom. You persecute entire communities. You have 2.3 million unemployed. You govern *your* society and we'll govern *ours*.' It was good, political knock-about, far from the usual Soviet politician's stock in trade and Westerners lapped it up. Margaret Thatcher even delivered an enthusiastic reference of her own: 'I like him. We can do business together.'

More interesting, though, was his decision, in June 1984, to attend the funeral of the head of the Italian Communist Party (PCI), Enrico Berlinguer. Berlinguer had been one of the fathers of the 'Eurocommunist' movement, which had freed itself from Moscow's attempts to keep it under Soviet control. The PCI, in particular, was not just one of the largest and most lively Communist parties in the world, it had also become increasingly critical of the Soviet regime, culminating in its 1982 declaration that the CPSU had exhausted the creative potential of the Bolshevik Revolution. As a result, Berlinguer and his party had become demonized in Moscow. Gorbachev, though, not only attended the funeral but hosted a dinner for senior Italian Communists where, much to their surprise, he announced that 'Berlinguer's criticism was not in vain.' It is perhaps not so surprising that Gorbachev should look to the PCI for some inspiration, though. From being a near-Stalinist party it had reformed itself to the point that it was close to becoming the largest political movement in Italy. It had shown itself able to remain true to basic socialist values about equality of opportunity while still encouraging a lively entrepreneurial culture in those regions and towns it controlled, and it had done this within a political system riddled with crime, corruption and patronage.

This was, therefore, not just a public relations campaign. During Chernenko's reign, Gorbachev began to develop not just his own political style but his own ideas as well. Of course, he could not go too far in publicly distancing himself from the official line, but he foreshadowed his future reformism in several ways. For a start, he began trying to reconcile Soviet rule and the realities of the market. Whereas Andropov had accepted that there was a need to offer workers incentives to work well, Gorbachev went further, noting that the Soviet government had to learn to use the tools of capitalism – 'such economic levers as prices, production cost, profit, credit and the like' – to manage its economy. Secondly, as he became more involved in foreign policy, so too did he try to give it a more constructive spin. Even when he was having to echo Chernenko's relatively confrontationalist line, Gorbachev introduced a note of optimism. While not directly contradicting the official view that East–West relations were worsening, he still affirmed his belief that they could be improved and that this was of vital importance to the USSR. Third, he continued his slow and often uncertain conversion to a belief in the need for an active, informed and above all independent 'civil society' whereby groups and individuals could play a part in politics. In a key address he made in December 1983, shortly after being given the politically important job of Central Committee Secretary for Ideology, he called for 'a more complete expression of the varied interests of the Soviet people...[and] a new impulse to the democratization of our social and intellectual life'.

To Western readers, this may not sound especially dramatic, but it needs to be considered in context. This was a man in the running to become General Secretary of the Communist Party of the Soviet Union. Even though the 1960s and 1970s had

come to see the CPSU dominated by men interested in administration and power politics rather than ideological zealots, they
were still tied to a belief that the market was an evil feature of
capitalism, that the West was working to destroy the Soviet
system and that the Party already spoke for the whole Soviet
people. Gorbachev's story is one of political growth, and thus
this represented another milestone on his journey, as he
publicly began questioning some of those mummified orthodoxies.

General Secretary Gorbachev

By early 1985, Chernenko was clearly terminally ill. Macabre
attempts to portray him as still in command only worsened the
impression. In February, for example, he was shown on Soviet
television purportedly casting his vote during elections.
Although he managed to say a few words and stand unaided,
most viewers were rather more conscious of the watchful aides
who hovered by him and the unusual appearance of the
'polling station', which turned out to be a hospital room decked
out for the cameras. Gorbachev, by contrast, put on a confident
performance worthy of a Western politician on the campaign
trail, turning up to vote with his family and joking with the
journalists as his granddaughter dropped his ballot in the box.
    At this eleventh hour, Chernenko was persuaded to adopt the
one tactic which really could hurt Gorbachev: trying to
cultivate a chosen successor of his own. He turned to Viktor
Grishin, the Party Secretary of Moscow, and a man in many
ways in his own mould. Grishin was a man of the *apparat*
through and through, and he appealed to the sizeable
constituency of leaders who feared the implications of reform
in general and renewed anti-corruption campaigns in
particular. He also acquired an unlikely ally in the form of
Grigori Romanov, the Party Secretary for Leningrad.
Romanov had been a member of the 'Andropov team' of sorts,
though representing its most authoritarian and uncompro-
mising wing. Romanov realized that change was necessary but
put all emphasis upon administrative reorganization and discipline. First and foremost, though, he was ambitious and only a

few years older than Gorbachev. He realized that if his (relatively) young rival won power, Romanov would never again be likely to be able to make a bid for the General Secretaryship. Much as the Andropovians had backed Chernenko in the full knowledge he soon would die, so too did Romanov come to support the 66-year-old Grishin as the older of two evils.

At 7:20 p.m. on 10 March 1985, Chernenko died. Three hours later the Politburo met to consider the succession and by the next evening, the USSR had a new General Secretary. The speed of the transition should not necessarily be seen as proof of the strength of Gorbachev's support. In many ways, quite the opposite was true, as matters were rushed with the intention of excluding supporters of Grishin's. Only nine voting members of the Politburo could make the meeting: with Gromyko chairing, four backed Grishin, four Gorbachev. Three could not reach Moscow in time to vote, although two – Vorotnikov and Kunayev – were able to make their views known via secure communications links. Vorotnikov declared for Gorbachev and Kunayev for Grishin. With the balance even, Gromyko was able to use his casting vote, which clinched the day for Gorbachev. This was a very close run election, though. Vladimir Shcherbitski, the Ukrainian Party Secretary, had been on an official visit to the USA. A convinced enemy of change, had he been able, he would undoubtedly have voted for Grishin. As things stood, Gorbachev had won, but only on the slenderest and most artificial of margins.

No time was wasted honouring Chernenko and the old ways he represented. The newspapers did not even print the traditional black-bordered picture of the dead leader on their front pages, instead carrying Gorbachev's photograph. Gorbachev's funeral oration was unprecedentedly short, even perfunctory, and dwelt more upon the challenges of the future than the triumphs of the past. What is more, Gorbachev used the occasion to announce a resumption of Andropov's campaigns, warning that he would 'fight all manifestations of humbug and sloganeering, arrogance and irresponsibility'. At the age of 54, he suddenly had thrust upon him the burden of centuries of backwardness and repression, decades of stagnation and cynicism and years of uncertainty and dashed hopes.

It is easy to damn Chernenko. He lacked Gorbachev's dynamic charisma, Andropov's cool intellect or even Brezhnev's political longevity. He was every inch a man of 1970s Soviet politics, a clubbable insider able to cobble together cosy deals and turn a pretty phrase to flatter Brezhnev. His misfortune was to come to power in 1984, at a time when the whole Soviet political order was in crisis and evolution. He was for sure guilty of a callous and short-termist disregard for the consequences of his actions, of an inability to appreciate the challenges facing his state and a stubborn and populist nationalism. But these are all classic features of that 1970s vintage *Homo Sovieticus*. Chernenko could have been far worse. He made no serious attempt to renounce his part of the deal with the reformists. Indeed, when Prime Minister Tikhonov made an early attempt to stop Gorbachev from chairing Politburo sessions in his absence, Chernenko promptly squashed it. A Party loyalist, Chernenko proved prepared to accept the rules and etiquette of Party discipline, and many of his more far-fetched initiatives could be reined in or limited. Gorbachev managed to talk him out of returning the name 'Stalingrad' to the Soviet map, while Gromyko managed to limit the damage caused by Chernenko's coolness towards the Chinese. Indeed, Chernenko did the reformists one real service. They had hoped he would do little and die soon; these he obligingly did, and with him he took to the grave any thought that the USSR and the Party could survive without reform.

Reading and Sources

Understandably, little serious attention has been paid to Chernenko, although Marc Zlotnik's article 'Chernenko succeeds', in *Problems of Communism*, volume 33, number 2 (1984), is useful, as is Ilya Zemtsov's biography, *Chernenko, the Last Bolshevik* (1989, Transaction). For a sense of the politics and policies of the era, John Parker's *Kremlin in Transition, volume 1* (1991, Unwin Hyman) again offers a meticulous reconstruction. Dusko Doder and Louise Branson's biography *Gorbachev: Heretic in the Kremlin* (1990, Futura) is quite good on these early years of central power, while the first public revelation of Andropov's abortive attempt to have Gorbachev accepted as his heir came from the first-class BBC television documentary series *The Second Russian Revolution.*

4

GORBACHEV THE TECHNOCRAT: *USKORENIYE* AND THE ATTEMPT TO MODERNIZE

Having begun with a very limited vision of reform, once in power Gorbachev's views were to change dramatically. After all, his early approach was one he inherited from Andropov. This presupposed that the system simply needing modernization, streamlining and discipline. Behind this was an essential belief in the existing order and a glib assumption that the USSR's underlying economic, social and political problems could be solved by managerial reforms. In many ways, the catch-phrase of the day said it all: *uskoreniye*, 'acceleration'. In other words, more speed, but no change in basic direction. Gorbachev would come to appreciate the enormity of the task facing him, though, and thus develop new strategies. Above all, he would come to question the direction of the USSR's process. The *uskoreniye* of the period 1985–6 would prove a disastrous failure; what it was accelerating the Soviet Union towards was not a glorious future but a precipice.

Consolidating Power

As discussed in the previous chapter, Gorbachev's election in March 1985 had been on the slenderest of margins. He thus came to power facing several severe handicaps. The mass of the bureaucracy, if accepting the intellectual case for reform, were deeply suspicious of anything which might threaten their powers or their comfortable lifestyle. Furthermore, although he had inherited the motley collection of reformists and puritans Andropov had assembled, Gorbachev did not have either absolute authority over them or a sizeable personal following. Brezhnev, for example, had surrounded himself with his 'Dnepropetrovsk Mafia' of cronies from his days as that city's Party Secretary. Gorbachev, by contrast, had risen too quickly and been too closely associated with Andropov to have much of a circle of personal clients.

His first priority thus had to be to consolidate his own position. At this he was startlingly successful. In part, he was the beneficiary both of Andropov's legacy and simple good luck, but he can also claim much of the credit himself. He was to prove a complete failure at the arts of open, democratic politics in the latter stages of his career, but he proved to be a master of behind-the-scenes political wheeling and dealing. Six weeks after his election, a plenum (meeting) of the Party's Central Committee confirmed the Politburo places of two of his closest allies of the time, Nikolai Ryzhkov and Yegor Ligachev. Most importantly, Ligachev retained his post as Central Committee Secretary for Organizational-Party Work. This department ran the *nomenklatura* system which controlled access to key jobs in the country and thus gave Gorbachev wide scope to sweep in a new generation of leaders and managers.

This he and Ligachev set to do with vigour. By the XXVII Party Congress in February 1986, some 40 per cent of key posts had new incumbents. Within a year, Gorbachev had replaced a third of government ministers and republican Party Secretaries. In July 1985, he managed to ease Foreign Minister Gromyko into a dignified but politically impotent retirement as President, a job which at this time was entirely ceremonial. In a surprising move, Gorbachev appointed Eduard Shevardnadze in his place. The former Interior Minister and then Party Secretary of Georgia, Shevardnadze had no experience of international diplomacy. Unlike so many of Gorbachev's appointments, though, this proved inspired. Shevardnadze was close to Gorbachev; back in December 1984 they had had a frank discussion of the problems facing the Soviet system and agreed that life 'had all gone rotten'. Like Gorbachev, Shevardnadze had benefited from Andropov's patronage. He was also a smooth and charming operator happy to endorse Gorbachev's newly flexible approaches to the West. In September, Ryzhkov became Chair of the Council of Ministers, in effect responsible for the daily running of the government. By early 1986, then, Gorbachev had been able to set his stamp upon the Soviet regime. The question was, what to do with that power?

Part of the problem for the reformers, but also one of the opportunities with which they were presented, was the very variety of rival approaches and initiatives. With Gorbachev busy developing both his power base and his ideas and Chernenko's fading energies devoted to a quick place in history, 1984–5 had seen the USSR drifting rudderless. It is thus hardly surprising that many other actors and institutions seized the opportunity to set out their own demands and ideas. As will be discussed more fully below, the military and its natural allies within the industrial sector (who manufactured the materiel the soldiers bought) tried to increase their already huge share of the national budget. At the same time, though, there were liberals who had made full use of the opportunities of the Chernenko era to develop their own platforms. One of Andropov's concerns had been to move away from the crass and counter-productive propaganda of the Brezhnev era and adopt a more sensitive and sophisticated approach to the management of news and information. As a result, he introduced new people into many of the departments responsible for censorship and the media, and it was during Chernenko's term that their presence first began to make itself felt. In February 1984, for example, the youth newspaper *Komsomol'skaya pravda* published an article called 'Duty' which for the first time broached the question of how the state was failing to look after injured veterans of the Afghan war. Conservatives promptly complained to the Party Secretariat's Ideology Department, which Suslov had made a bastion of censors and bigots. The department had since been entrusted to Arkadi Vol'sky and Yegor Ligachev, though, both members of the 'Andropov team'. They drew up a resolution supporting the article and persuaded an admittedly reluctant Chernenko to sign it. Slowly but irresistibly, *glasnost'*, 'openness', was on the way.

The 'Human Factor' and the Dilemmas of Economic Reform

Yet Gorbachev saw his first priority as economic reform. One of the underlying themes of the Gorbachev era is the failure of the Kremlin leadership ever to understand, much less master, the intricate and bizarre economics of the Soviet system. While in theory almost everything was planned by the centre, in practice economic managers routinely ignored or misled Moscow, confident that a little bribery and a lot of confusion could keep their activities hidden. There was also a huge underground 'shadow economy', which accounted for anything between 10 and 40 per cent of the total, and which often overlapped with the legal economy as, for example, goods were stolen for re-sale or managers found on the black market necessary resources or spare parts they could not obtain legally. What is more, the Soviet elite almost by definition knew very little about economics. Although a relative handful of academics had managed to keep up to date with theory by studying Western systems, most members of the *nomenklatura* were never taught sensible supply-and-demand economics. Given their privileged lifestyles, they never even had to cope with the day-to-day haggling and trading by which ordinary Soviet citizens got by. Economics would be one of Gorbachev's blind spots, and ultimately a crucial one.

For all that, he did come to power with a clear understanding that the USSR was suffering because its economy was not only lagging behind that of the West but also failing to meet the needs of either the elite or the masses. He wanted quick results, and introduced a series of measures intended to produce them. In fact, they proved disastrous, largely because they were based upon an inadequate grasp of the problem and a lack of suitable tools with which to repair the system. The basic ideas behind his approach were simple and apparently sensible. He wanted to reward good practice and hard work and at the same time crack down on laziness, out-of-date methods and counter-productive habits. The underlying assumption was that the main problem had less to do with the very foundations of the Soviet planned economy but with the bad habits of the Soviet people. Workers and managers alike simply needed to be shown that they could no longer hold on to their lax old habits, to, as he said over and again, 'activate the human factor'. To this end he introduced a series of policies which only worsened matters:

- Higher targets. Over the protests of the economists of *Gosplan*, the next Five Year Plan (1986–90) featured dramatically increased production targets. It called for annual increases in national income of 4.1 per cent, well above preceding levels.
- Streamlining the bureaucracy by bringing ministries under the co-ordination of new 'superministerial' bodies. In November 1985, for example, six other bodies were merged into the agriculture super-ministry *Gosagroprom*. In practice, this simply created yet another layer of bureaucracy.
- *Gospriemka*, a new campaign for quality control. Shoddy goods which would previously have been dumped on the market instead were rejected by inspectors, and factories and workers were penalized for it. Some 20 per cent of output was rejected, but with the plan targets being so high factories lacked the time and raw materials to make up this shortfall. The supply of goods to Soviet consumers (who would generally rather have had a substandard item than not to have one at all), thus actually fell. Besides which, workers failed to win the pay bonuses to which they had become accustomed, leading to a growing problem of labour unrest. In a vicious circle, this led to a further reduction of production and quality and not surprisingly this campaign was allowed to drop after 1988.

After all, modernizing a system and people's attitudes is an expensive business. It is expensive in terms of money, in that it requires investment in new technology and retraining as well as bonuses for those who work well or hard. It is expensive in terms of production, in that workers have to be given time to retrain and plants need to be closed down or slowed up in order to be refitted. It is expensive in terms of time, in that new ideas and ways of working need to be introduced slowly and do not become habit overnight. It is also politically expensive; people tend to fear and mistrust the new, and they need either to be forced to change or else convinced that it is in their best interests. Even Stalin, who used quite astonishing brutality in his drive to industrialize the USSR, also understood that positive incentives were also necessary, and offered money, advancement and prestige to the 'heroes of production'.

In both the short and long term, the implications of this initial campaign for economic reform were catastrophic. By increasing production targets in the 1986–90 plan, Gorbachev ensured that for almost his entire time in office the Soviet economy would be working flat out. There would never be that vital breathing space in which to modernize, and instead workers and managers alike associated reform with unfeasibly high targets and frantic overwork. There were almost no positive incentives for success. Given the under-investment which had characterized most of the Soviet economy, *Gospriemka* ensured that even hard-working and efficient enterprises were unlikely to win their bonuses. What is more, a campaign against 'unearned incomes' in 1986, intended as a broadside against the embezzlers and bribe-takers who were bleeding the official economy and making life harder for those who did want to make a go of honest private business, similarly ended up only hurting those it was meant to encourage. The truly criminal carried on paying off the police and the local Party bosses, and instead the targets became the relative handful of genuine entrepreneurs, the very same people who would have been expected to have become the seedcorn of a new commercial middle class. This was bitterly remembered when Gorbachev later introduced more serious efforts to encourage grassroots capitalism. A glance at the state of post-Soviet Russia in the 1990s shows that the new entrepreneurs tend to come not from this generation but the very same criminals and corrupt officials who had bought themselves immunity in 1986.

The Anti-Alcohol Campaign

Perhaps the best example of Gorbachev's mishandling of the 'human factor' and the way badly-thought-through reforms actually worsened matters is the anti-alcohol campaign he launched in May 1985. Again, this stemmed from a possibly well-meant but undoubtedly naive idea nonetheless betraying a real lack of understanding and sympathy with the views of ordinary citizens. Unable to protest openly against a regime they felt had betrayed them, increasing numbers had turned to the bottle for solace. The consumption of strong drink (over 40 per cent proof) rose to the highest in the world. This was not only indicative of widespread disillusion, but it was a real problem for the economy. Productivity was suffering, perhaps by as much as 10 per cent, as workers turned up drunk, drank at work or took time out to nurse their hangovers. The hospitals were full of cases of alcohol poisoning and the police spent their nights sweeping up the drunks and locking them in drying-out cells. Perhaps a million alcoholics needed hospital treatment each year, while drunk drivers accounted for an annual toll of 14 000 traffic deaths. Like Andropov, but unlike those prodigious tipplers Brezhnev and Chernenko (and indeed, his eventual successor, Boris Yeltsin), Gorbachev was no great drinker. Besides, he was a believer in the system. He saw alcoholism as an offence to the Soviet ideal and a symptom of weak personal morals rather than a failing of the Soviet order. Gorbachev thus instituted an anti-alcohol campaign, designed to wean Soviet citizens from the bottle and teach them instead the rewards of moderation.

As with every other campaign, though, the stick was much more in evidence than the carrot. A few token gestures were made towards setting up education programmes and opening a few coffee and fruit juice bars where young people could meet as an alternative to beer halls. On the whole, though, this was an exercise which depended on a barrage of propaganda and coercion. Vineyards, breweries and vodka factories were closed, the opening hours of alcohol shops were limited and the police adopted a much more aggressive approach to public drunkenness. It was a challenge to the drinking habits of the Soviet people to rival the Prohibition of 1920s USA, a challenge the state was bound to lose. People turned instead to the black market and to *samogon*, a destructively potent home-brewed liquor. To distil their *samogon*, they raided the shops for sugar, leading to a country-wide shortage which even led to rationing.

After decades of it, the propaganda was something they found easy to ignore.

The campaign was not just a failure, it was a disaster. Instead of fairly pure vodka, drinkers turned to *samogon* and such other desperate sources of alcohol as perfume and anti-freeze. Incidences of poisoning actually increased, putting a greater burden on to an already over-stretched health service. What is more, the state had come to rely upon its earnings as the country's only legal producer of alcohol. By 1982, alcohol taxes made up fully 12 per cent of the entire state budget. As legal sales dwindled, not only did vast amounts of money flow into the black economy, swelling the profits of the Soviet Union's criminals and illegal entrepreneurs, but the government was forced to print more money to make up for its lost tax earnings. The more money that was printed, the greater the level of inflation. The official currency become ever-more worthless (a bottle of vodka could buy you a lot more than 10 times its notional value in rubles), and the campaign only deepened suspicions that 'reform' simply meant more work and less play.

The Thaw: Gorbachev and the Cold War

It may seem that there can scarcely be a greater contrast between Gorbachev's clumsy, poorly informed and counter-productive economic policies and his polished mastery of inter-national diplomacy. He realized from the first that success in foreign policy could have very positive implications for his domestic politics. It could encourage and pacify a population otherwise frustrated by the pain of reform. It might allow him to transfer resources from the defence budget to economic restructuring and the provision of consumer goods. It could also lead to greater trade and access to the Western credits and technology which would make that economic restructuring so much easier. Even so, while he was to shine as a world statesman, his foreign policies ultimately did not help his bid to reform the USSR. If anything, they were to contribute to his downfall, by alienating the nationalist and conservative wing of the Party. Besides which, his new proposals and concessions were not necessarily all that new. Many were repackaged versions of previous initiatives. More often, Gorbachev was simply putting into practice suggestions which had been made before but which no leader had dared or wanted to adopt. Nevertheless, it is true that not only did Gorbachev go much further than his predecessors, but he also tried to give these different initiatives some underlying cohesion. In many ways, he had no alternative but to try to end the Cold War and reduce nuclear arsenals; the USSR's economic and political weaknesses dictated it. But more than just the cynical retreat of a defeated power, this became part of a wider campaign to create a more collaborative world order. In it, the USSR would deal with other powers not so much as rivals but fellow tenants of 'our common home' as he, at various times, called Europe, Asia and the Earth as a whole. On one level this sounds like so much bland rhetoric, but there was real conviction behind it. Gorbachev was a lawyer by training and wanted to see a world bound by sensible codes of conduct. He was also a deal-maker by nature and preferred to create a world in which he could haggle and persuade rather than one locked in military confrontation.

From the beginning, Gorbachev signalled his intention to concentrate on international relations. A month after his election, he announced a unilateral suspension of nuclear weapons tests and a freeze on the deployment of intermediate-range nuclear missiles. On one level, this was an essentially symbolic gesture as testing could be resumed at any time, and even without these new missiles the USSR had a formidable arsenal. But gestures are important in politics, especially when followed up by evidence that they are more than purely empty. In July 1985, Shevardnadze replaced Gromyko as Foreign Minister, while in October Gorbachev proposed across the board 50 per cent cuts in US and Soviet nuclear stockpiles. Next month, he met US President Reagan at Geneva. Nothing of substance was agreed at the summit, but Gorbachev had the opportunity to demonstrate his diplomatic finesse and begin to develop his personal relationship with Reagan.

Although it was important to begin to woo the Americans, Gorbachev faced a rather more immediate and formidable obstacle in dealing with the resistance of his own military–industrial complex. The position of the military and their allies within the defence industries was ambiguous. On the one hand, they had welcomed Andropov's and then Gorbachev's commitments to modernizing the economy. In this they followed the lead of Marshal Nikolai Ogarkov, Chief of the General Staff between 1977 and 1984. In contrast to the tank and infantry officers who usually dominated the High Command, Ogarkov was an engineer and especially worried by the technological gap opening up between the USSR and the West. When Andropov began proposing arms reduction treaties with NATO, though, Ogarkov dared to disagree. To a large extent, his interventions were crucial in burying any hopes of an agreement on intermediate-range missiles in Europe in 1983. He was a constant and vocal lobbyist for not smaller but greater defence budgets. When Chernenko came to power, he tried again, doing all he could to talk up the military threat from the West. 'Never before,' he told a General Staff conference, 'has the ideological and economic struggle, still less US and NATO military preparations, acquired such an all-encompassing and menacing a nature.' When even Chernenko refused to spend any more money on the military, Ogarkov even drew parallels with the period just before the Nazi invasion of the USSR during the Second World War. This was going too far; the political leadership decided to make of him an example to reaffirm their control over the military and even other generals feared he was becoming a liability. In September 1984, he was transferred out of his politically sensitive post.

Nevertheless, Ogarkov had set the tone for the military. They were in favour of modernization and a revitalization of the Party so long as this meant a more dynamic economy, more advanced weapons and healthier and more committed recruits. They did not see or would not accept that reform would have to be paid for by a transfer of resources from defence to consumer goods or that a necessary part of political liberalization would be freedom of the press to point out military blunders and idiocies. Like so many others who had benefited from Brezhnev 'golden years', they refused to accept that the days were over when the state could spend and spend without concern for the debts it was accumulating. Unlike most of his predecessors, Gorbachev had no army experience or even close contacts with soldiers. He thus lacked patience with his generals and soon realized that he would have to rely on out-manoeuvring rather than persuading them.

He had probably had a hand in the dismissal of Ogarkov and his replacement by General Sergei Akhromeyev, a relatively sensible and flexible military thinker. His first opportunity as General Secretary, though, came in May 1985, when several long-serving members of the High Command retired, in some cases after more than a little encouragement. At the same time, Gorbachev began preparing the ground for an eventual withdrawal from Afghanistan. The army was told to begin scaling down its combat operations and concentrate on minimizing its losses and holding existing ground rather than any new offensives, something borne out by the fall in Soviet casualties, from 2343 in 1984 down to 1868 in 1985. Later, as Gorbachev became more and more desperate to clinch arms deals with the USA, his relations with the military were to become steadily worse, but from the very first it is clear that the High Command, while anxious to see the USSR modernized, was very wary of Gorbachev and his talk of wider reforms.

The Failure of *Uskoreniye*: Gorbachev's Slow Awakening

Counter-productive and unsuccessful reforms are worse than no reforms at all, and the mistakes of *uskoreniye* certainly contributed to the steady decline of the USSR. A fragile and inefficient but nonetheless just about working economic system was put under increasing pressure by reforms which failed to reflect the genuine needs of change. Expectations were raised to levels no reforms could attain, making disappointment and disillusion inevitable. Gorbachev's initial 'honeymoon' with the Soviet people, not least the result of a sense of relief at having a presentable leader not yet of pensionable age at the helm, soon soured thanks to his decision to crank the economy into high gear and his anti-alcohol campaign. He could not even afford to keep them happy by buying in consumer goods from abroad; declining world prices for Soviet oil, coal and gas exports forced a cut in imports to the tune of 8 billion rubles. The Soviet elite began a process of fragmentation, as many dug in their heels against reform, while others – most notably the new Party Secretary of Moscow, Boris Yeltsin – saw the opportunities in championing it. Given the concentration of power in the hands of his elite and the extent to which Gorbachev depended upon them to carry out his plans, this was to prove a central problem for him.

Of course, with hindsight it is relatively easy to criticize Gorbachev's first attempt to reform the USSR. It is probably fair, though, also to note that it could hardly have been otherwise. Gorbachev did not have the personal power base from which to go about bringing dramatic change to the country. Instead, he had to devote much of his energy to consolidating his position and trying to convince his peers and the Soviet bureaucratic elite as a whole of the need for change – something in which he was only ever partly successful. Secondly, he had very few usable tools and options at his disposal. With the budget already in the red, he could not throw money at his problems. With the Soviet people disillusioned and the *nomenklatura* complacent, he could not rely on either. Disengaging from the Cold War and unlearning the habits of the past would both take time and effort. Finally, Gorbachev himself could hardly have dreamt of the scale and complexity of the problems facing him. How could he? He had been raised in a system which demanded obedience to the Party line and orthodoxy. A member of the privileged elite, he had been spared many of the hardships and deceits which were part of most Soviets' daily grind. Now he was General Secretary, he was bombarded with data and analyses, much of which was either bogus or irredeemably biased. The only way Gorbachev would learn the need for more substantial – and above all political – reform was by the failure of less ambitious programmes.

Unfortunately, in the process Gorbachev lost sight of another basic truth: that providing the Soviet people with a say in their future would only work to his advantage if he could convince them that his programme offered them not only the best future relations, but a genuine turnaround of the USSR's economic decline. It would also require measures to ensure that the fruits of any such success made its way to the masses, and not into a reflation of the defence budget or the perks of the *nomenklatura*. The tragedy is that as Gorbachev became increasingly aware of the need for political reform, he failed to appreciate the need for parallel successful economic reform. Thus, for all he spoke about the 'human factor', ultimately Gorbachev never really understood it.

Reading and Sources

John Miller's *Mikhail Gorbachev and the End of Soviet Power* has a particularly good angle on Gorbachev's character and ideals, while Rachel Walker's *Six Years That Shook the World* clearly outlines the flaws inherent in *uskoreniye*. From an economist's perspective, Anders Aslund's *Gorbachev's Struggle for Economic Reform* is a particularly effective study of the early years of change. Martin Walker's *The Waking Giant* (1987, Abacus), even if in hindsight ludicrously over-optimistic, is an intelligent and very readable summary of the high hopes generated by Gorbachev's accession to power.

As regards specific issues covered in this chapter Stephen White's *Russia Goes Dry* is an exhaustive study of the whole ridiculous anti-alcohol campaign, while the best study of the politics surrounding the dismissal of Marshal Ogarkov is Dale Herspring's The Soviet High Command (1990, Princeton University Press) (which also has much to say about the High Command's politics throughout this period). David Lane's edited collection *Elites and Political Power in the USSR* contains several articles looking at the very specific nuts and bolts issues of Gorbachev's struggle with the CPSU elite, notably those in part one.

5

GORBACHEV THE RERFORMER: *GLASNOST'* AND *PERESTROIKA*

At the XXVII Party Congress, in February and March 1986, Gorbachev declared that what the country and the CPSU needed was nothing short of 'radical reform'. This might have sounded like so much rhetoric, but in many ways this Congress represented another milestone in Gorbachev's personal political growth. From the public politics of the podium and in the intense behind-the-scenes preparation and negotiations which took place, a new willingness to liberalize the USSR began to emerge. *Uskoreniye*, the politics of simple economic modernization, gave way to the much more broadly based processes of comprehensive *perestroika* (restructuring) and *glasnost'* (openness).

After all, up to this point Gorbachev had believed in change, in modernization and in restoring some honesty and pride to the Soviet system. But he had seen this almost exclusively as something coming from the top of the system. The role of the Soviet people (and, indeed, the majority of the *nomenklatura*) was simply to follow this new line and become dutifully enthusiastic, sober and hard-working Soviet patriots. In this he was betraying all the traits of the traditional Soviet leader. All official pronouncements stressed the 'leading role' of the Party, which seemingly lay behind every Soviet success. Government was built around the notion of planning, that every aspect of the economic, political and social life of the country could be managed from Moscow. It was not only factories which had plans: policeman had arrest quotas to meet, soldiers fighting in

Afghanistan had performance indices to match and even social clubs were established not where there was a demand but where centrally established formulas dictated. Indeed, this way of governing was older even than the Soviet regime. Until its overthrow in 1917, tsarist Russia had been a country of tight state control, imposed by an often brutal and corrupt civil service and aristocracy.

Like Andropov, Gorbachev had at first tried simply to use the old machinery of government to reform. One of the main reasons why this failed was that the old machinery, the old ways of running the USSR, were a very large part of the problem. Thanks, to a large extent, to certain of his advisers, Gorbachev slowly began to realize that rather than seeing the Soviet people as the problem and the bureaucracy as the solution, it was more the other way round. As early as February 1986, the Party newspaper *Pravda*, in an article which must at least have been sanctioned by the government, was talking about an 'immobile, inert and tenacious "party-administrative system"'. All this did not make Gorbachev a 'democrat', only a 'democratizer'. In other words, he did not believe that the people had the moral and absolute right to govern themselves through their own elected representatives. It was only much later, for example, that he would countenance the idea of candidates from organized blocs other than the CPSU standing in elections. But it did mean that he began granting the Soviet people an increased say in many of the practical aspects of their day-to-day lives, albeit still within a system run by the Communist Party: a greater freedom of speech, for example, new opportunities for individual economic activity, even the chance to establish local pressure groups.

This may not sound like much, but as soon as Gorbachev began such limited democratization, three interlinked processes which would ultimately tear the USSR apart began to emerge:

- Having been permitted to shed part of the state control imposed on them during 70 years of Party rule and centuries of tsarism, the Soviet people came to expect and demand an ever greater say in their lives. When the Party proved unable or unwilling to meet their new expectations (ranging from greater personal freedoms to a better standard of living), they looked instead to new leaders and answers, from nationalists to liberals, from environmentalism to the Church.

• Vested interests within the Party became ever more alarmed by democratization. For the wrong reasons, they nonetheless had a more realistic notion of just how dangerous this could be to the Party and the whole Soviet system. Freer speech may not sound like much, for example, but what happens when people use it to criticize the Party? Gorbachev glibly assumed that pluralism would be purely to his advantage, yet he would discover that freedoms could as easily be used against, as for, his programmes.

• Gorbachev and many other reformists would themselves be radicalized, as will be discussed later. The greater the degree of change they tried to bring to the system, both the greater the resistance of the conservatives and the harder their task would be.

Glasnost' and the Beginnings of Political Reform

Generally translated as 'openness', though perhaps more accurately 'speaking out', *glasnost'* became a central part of Gorbachev's idea of reform, and one in which he showed his ability to go beyond Andropov's limitations. The word was not a new one in Soviet and, indeed, Russian politics. Brezhnev had used (if never practised) it, while Andropov had tried to change the way the Soviet state's official media communicated to the people, by doing away with the most blatant propaganda and allowing greater leeway for different commentators to present the facts in different ways. This fell far short of believing that the people had any right to the truth or that there was any advantage for the state in keeping the population informed. It was just that Andropov knew full well how far most citizens mistrusted the official line and relied instead on gossip and third-hand retellings of the news from the Russian-language services of the BBC or the US government's Radio Liberty stations. Khrushchev, when he was General Secretary in the 1950s, had authorized publication of the book *A Day in the Life of Ivan Denisovich* because its portrayal of the inhuman-ities of the Gulag labour camps made it a useful weapon with which it to attack the reputation of his predecessor, Stalin. So too did Andropov try to manage the media to his advantage, not least by leaking tales of the corruption of Brezhnev and other members of the Old Guard.

Gorbachev was a politician, and as such he understood the value of media manipulation as well as any Western 'spin doctor'. He was certainly not above using the media to his advantage, whether staging good photo opportunities or smearing his opponents. As during Andropov's reign, news of corruption trials was used to undermine the remaining members of Brezhnev's circle. But he went well beyond such limited and pragmatic liberalization and presided over an astonishing explosion in public and media freedoms. He did so for four main reasons. First of all, he realized that he needed the support of the literary and cultural intelligentsia – writers, artists, journalists, film directors, dramatists – to convince both the elite and the masses that the country needed major reform, a slow and painful process. He needed to break through the complacency and cynicism created by the old propaganda. The elite needed to be made aware of just how serious the danger facing the Party and the USSR really was, and how far it was in their long-term interest to help Gorbachev reform the country. Better, went the subtext, the loss of a few powers, perks and privileges to save the system than risk losing them all if reform fails. As for the masses, they needed to be persuaded that they had some hope for the future, some reason to accept the extra burdens of reform. To an extent, this was another trade-off. Instead of lying to them but buying them off with a comfortable lifestyle, as had happened in the early 1970s, the masses would instead be treated like responsible adults and told the truth about the country's plight. In return, though, they would have to shoulder a greater responsibility for doing something about the problem.

Secondly, Gorbachev began to realize that he could not rely on his control over the bureaucracy and the information it fed him. A month after his election, for example, he had made a supposedly surprise walkabout in Moscow, in the course of which city officials suggested he drop in on a 'typical young couple' to see how they lived. The apartment was clean and large, the couple attentive and optimistic, telling him just what he hoped and wanted to hear. It was only half way through that he noticed the Central Committee logo on the china. A furious Gorbachev realized that he had been set up. No head of government ever makes a totally 'surprise' visit – there are security checks to be made, local grandees to be invited, routes to be planned. As soon as they heard of the plan, the city author-ities had arranged a little spectacle for the General Secretary, both to convince him of how well they were doing their jobs and because traditionally that had been what most Soviet leaders had expected. Indeed, this had been going on for centuries. When, in the eighteenth century, Tsarina Catherine the Great had decided to see her country by river cruise, her favourite, Count Potemkin, secretly arranged for prosperous-looking villages to be built along her route. These 'Potemkin villages' were just empty shells, populated by peasants from elsewhere brought in and spruced up just for the day, but Catherine was well-pleased and, in effect, a tradition was established.

It was thus all very well trying to use *glasnost'* to try and win over the *apparatchiki*, but Gorbachev could not depend upon this. He needed also his own information sources and a means of exerting his authority over the bureaucracy. For this he took a time-honoured Soviet method and gave it a distinctively Gorbachevian twist. Lenin had always been a keen advocate of the use of the working class as a check on the bureaucrats, while Stalin had more crudely made great use of denunciations to eliminate his political enemies. Gorbachev saw *glasnost'* as a way to create a nation of whistle-blowers who would work with him to keep the *apparatchiki* in line.

Not that *glasnost'* only meant that the masses could now inform on their bureaucratic masters. The third aspect of the policy was that it allowed – indeed, encouraged – far more open debate within the elite as to possible reforms. Again, this reflects both Gorbachev's own political style and his growing political maturity. By nature, he preferred to be in the centre rather than necessarily leading from the front, the man able to tip the balance in favour of one camp or another. This meant that he was able to play off different groups against each other but also that he could quickly shift his position as circumstances dictated. This is, after all, part of the reason why he cultivated both rivals Andropov and Suslov as patrons during his rise to power, just as he would later try to play off conservatives and radicals within the Party. In addition, he did realize just how far he needed both to protect his fragile political position and also find new approaches to reform after the failure of *uskoreniye*. In a very neat way, *glasnost'* offered him a central position, some political security and new ideas all at once. He started debates, typically by introducing some new buzzword such as *perestroika* ('restructuring') or *demokratizatsiya* ('democratization'), which could mean almost anything. Then he sat back and let intellectuals, managers, radicals and conservatives come up with their own definitions, engage in coded debates in the pages of the Party press and generally worry away at it. Gorbachev could sit aloof from all this, assess the ideas that were being raised and the political currents at work, before stepping in and adopting one line of argument as his own.

Glasnost' and Government

Underlying all three previous points is the fourth, most general and most powerful argument: a system of government which excessively limits and distorts information flows is one which cannot evolve. Information flows are a vital part of government, whether vertical (between rulers and ruled) or horizontal (between different regions, groups and interests). Economic development, for example, was being delayed by the strict security conditions under which so many scientists and engineers had to work. In many instances, they were even prohibited from talking with colleagues in other offices, even though so many of the technological breakthroughs of the late twentieth century have been precisely the result of people crossing traditional disciplinary boundaries and sharing ideas. Even the humble photocopier was seen not as a means of increasing the spread of information but, since it could be used to copy subversive underground newsletters, a threat to the security of the state. Every one had to be registered with the local police, and detailed records kept of every copy made, by whom, for whom and why.

The extent to which the Soviet Union's cult of secrecy had become counter-productive was best illustrated by the Chernobyl' nuclear disaster of 26 April 1986. Early that Saturday morning, an explosion ripped through its nuclear reactor number 4, destroying part of the control room and sending a plume of radioactive smoke high into the atmosphere. The Chernobyl' nuclear power station comprised four such RBMK reactors, and so the first battle was to prevent the ensuing fire from spreading to the other three. With Kiev, the capital of the Ukraine, only about 130 kilometres away, there was a real threat to this city of two and a half million souls. The heroism of many in the emergency services cannot be doubted. Firemen and soldiers in many cases knowingly exposed themselves to lethal doses of radiation in the operation. But for days this life-and-death struggle to prevent the fire from spreading and the reactor from contaminating the water table took place behind a thick wall of secrecy.

Less than four and a half hours after the initial explosion, the Kremlin had been fully informed and the emergency response began. By Saturday evening, over 1000 victims of radiation poisoning had been identified and yet no public announcement was made. The decision was not even taken to evacuate the nearby town of Pripyat until late the next morning. Only on Monday morning did the government finally make a statement, and that only because the drifting clouds of radiation had reached Scandinavia, and the Swedes were about to issue a radiation alert. In a crisis, old habits reasserted themselves. Unsure of the scale of the disaster and the possible reaction of the people in the area, Gorbachev stayed silent. While thousands of troops were being brought in, while the entire Ukrainian medical services were being mobilized and while the air force was literally burying the still-burning reactor in thousands of tonnes of lead, sand and boron, Gorbachev stayed silent.

The practical consequences of the disaster were significant: in all, some 8000 died as a direct consequence, while the initial clean-up operation alone cost an already over-stretched budget the equivalent of $2.7 billion. Yet Chernobyl' also shocked Gorbachev into action. First of all, he was shocked that such a disaster could ever happen. It turned out to be the result of an experiment gone awry, which the local managers did not dare report in its early stages, when it could have been controlled. In short, it was a classic example of the problems bred by internal secrecy and the elite's traditional mistrust of and lack of concern for the people. Gorbachev also seems to have been taken aback, at his own response, at the way he so quickly abandoned any pretence of *glasnost'* when a crisis erupted. He did not come out of Chernobyl' very well although, politician to the last, he did what he could to turn it to his advantage. He used it to underline the dangers of nuclear weapons, for example, as part of his campaign to convince the West of the need for arms cuts. But beyond this, Chernobyl' seems to have shown him that *glasnost'* had to be a process: a philosophy of governing the country rather than a convenient tactic to use in some situations but not in others. By preaching openness and then by acting so secretively over Chernobyl' he had damaged his reputation and alienated a Soviet people who needed to be convinced that reform was more than just a new propaganda campaign.

Henceforth, disasters and blunders alike would be reported promptly and relatively honestly, such as the sinking of the ferry ship *Admiral Nakhimov* or the Armenian earthquake of 1988. Less obviously, but of greater long-term importance, the press was granted ever greater freedom to investigate the hitherto taboo issues, from the safety of the USSR's other reactors to the waste of public money by the Party. The summer of 1986 saw a veritable 'revolution of the journalists', as commentators and reporters began to test these new-found freedoms, to be followed by writers and artists and even academics. At last they were able honestly to consider such 'blank pages' in Soviet history as Stalin's purges and the execution of the last Tsar and his family in 1918.

Of course, it would take time for them to become used to such freedoms, but 1986 saw the first evidence that *glasnost'* meant more independence within the media rather than just more sophisticated state control. The veteran Petr Demichev was transferred from his job as Minister of Culture, and in June Gorbachev held a private meeting with key representatives of the cultural intelligentsia. He encouraged them to push *glasnost'* to its limits and, tellingly, appealed for their help against the conservative bureaucracy and against the entrenched habits of decades of secrecy. They responded with eagerness and alacrity. That month, the Union of Writers held a Congress which elected a new governing board including radical writers such as Chingiz Aitmatov (whose later novel *Plakha* would explore such hot issues as drug abuse and the disillusion of Soviet Central Asians) and Sergei Zalygin, the editor of the literary journal *Novy mir*. Under the limited cultural reform of the Khrushchev era, *Novy mir* had been a trailblazer, publishing *A Day in the Life of Ivan Denisovich*. Zalygin was to revive these traditions, even going on to publish works overtly critical of the Soviet legacy such as George Orwell's *1984*. Within the next year, a special commission restored thousands of previously banned books to the shelves and a whole new generation of truly critical and investigative films and television programmes emerged. The documentary *Is it Easy to be Young?* (1987) painted a picture of an angry and alienated youth culture, for example, while even the previously staid television networks began to look at Soviet life in the raw rather than purely retailing the propaganda image.

Informals: the Beginnings of the 'Revolution from Below'

A more telling sign that Gorbachev really understood that a corollary of *glasnost'* was greater individual and collective freedoms for the Soviet people was the rise of the 'informal movement'. Since the Stalin era, the Party had in effect reserved the right to manage all forms of organized social activity, from sports clubs to discussion groups. After Chernobyl', though, Gorbachev decided to relax controls on such groups and in July 1987 began explicitly admitting that reform was not simply a campaign for economic modernization but a social process which would ultimately stand or fall on the involvement of the Soviet people as a whole. Although it was not until the 1990 Law on Public Associations was passed that they acquired full legal status, in late 1986 it became clear that the regime was now prepared to free up this most basic level of organization from political control. Indeed, in some ways it actually encouraged it, by allowing groups which registered with the local authorities to set up joint bank accounts, carry out limited fundraising and even express political views. It needs to be stressed just how limited this last point was. These *neformaly*, or 'informals', were meant to steer clear of organized political action; they were certainly not meant to become parties to rival the CPSU. Nonetheless, Gorbachev was aware that this was a political act. Allowing, for example, environmentalists to band together to fight the construction of a new power station meant allowing them to become politically active given that it was the state which decided where it would be built and which would have to make any change of plan.

According to official figures, by the end of 1987 there were some 30 000 *neformaly* across the USSR, involving millions of people. While most were essentially leisure organizations, up to a quarter were either lobby groups (such as the Afghan veterans' clubs) or were involved in issues such as environmentalism which gave them an implicitly political function. This was the Soviet peoples' first real evidence that reform did not just mean a new policy from the top, but new opportunities for them to begin to play a part in shaping their future, and many leapt at the chance.

From Gorbachev's perspective, the informal movement was more than just a necessary part of *glasnost'*. It fitted in with his own growing belief that the Party's complete control over Soviet life was not only economically disadvantageous but a check upon the ability of the Soviet people to grow into their full personal and political maturity. This was quite a turnabout for a man raised within a system which elevated collective control over independent autonomy and suggests how far Gorbachev's ambitious and assertive character made him more sympathetic than any of his predecessors towards the ambitions of his people. At this time, though, Gorbachev's views were only beginning to change. *Glasnost'* and the informal movement were not intended to weaken the power of the Party but only to strengthen the reformers within it and assist them in their efforts. It also worked to the advantage of the educated middle class rather than the blue-collar masses. Nevertheless, it had dramatic implications for the future. More active citizens were given the first opportunities to organize and begin to articulate points of view opposed to the Party line. It is no coincidence that many of the radical and nationalist movements and parties which would tear the USSR apart had their beginnings in the *neformaly*. In addition, as *glasnost'* acquired its own momentum, it increasingly worked in ways Gorbachev could neither predict nor control. Even those groups which formed in support of *perestroika* would eventually form the basis for Boris Yeltsin's radical challenge to Gorbachev.

Reforming the Economy from the Grassroots

The same desire to cut back on over-centralization and open up opportunities for small-scale initiative was visible in the economic reforms introduced in this period, chiefly the 1987 Law on State Enterprises and the 1988 Law on Co-operatives. The former was drafted to give farm and factory managers and workers much greater autonomy from the centre, with workers encouraged to elect their managers. The Law on Co-operatives legalized a wide range of small businesses, from shops and restaurants through to after-school tutors and car mechanics. These could fix their own prices and were wholly independent of the plan. They would typically charge more than their state equivalents but offer greater quality and service. After all, their members were often working for a share of the profit rather than just for a fixed wage.

In theory, these initiatives would have introduced more motivation and market responsiveness to the economy. Workers could refuse to re-elect inefficient or unreconstructed managers, while factory managers and co-operatives, spying a demand, could move to meet it. In practice, it did nothing of the sort. Over-driven by an excessively ambitious plan, workers not surprisingly elected managers who offered an easy life and large bonuses (and promptly charged the cost back to government subsidies). In a planned, state-controlled economy, piecemeal reform is rarely sensible, especially when it has to be enforced by a bureaucracy which has no interest in doing so. Suspicious of the possible threat a new entrepreneurial middle class could pose, the *apparatchiki* tried to strangle the co-operative movement in a noose of red tape, excessive tax demands and non-collaboration. While many fell by the wayside, by the end of 1988, this sector employed over three-quarters of a million out of a total workforce of 135 million. Even so, these tended to be in the service sector, rather than actually making anything. Those who prospered did so because they were especially resourceful, they had a skill or commodity much in demand, or they knew how to buy protection from within the *apparat*. As for the Law on State Enterprises, without private banks from which to acquire investment capital, without a free market in raw materials and labour, without the profit motive and the threat of closure or sacking, managers rarely had the incentive or the opportunity to change their ways.

After all, the USSR's economic problems were terrifyingly deeply rooted, and the lesson of the 1990s seems to be that much of the Soviet industrial base could not have been reformed, only allowed to collapse and then rebuilt afresh. By October 1988, 24 000 out of 46 000 state enterprises were officially loss-makers. Were they to be closed, the USSR – a country whose constitution granted every citizen the right to a job – would suddenly have had to cope with perhaps 20 million unemployed. Gorbachev could not and would not go to such extreme lengths. Nor could he yet even try to tackle basic problems, such as the level of the budget deficit and the amount of money the government was paying to subsidize prices which bore little resemblance to true costs, but were being maintained at fixed levels for political reasons. Rents had not risen since 1928, for example.

Despite his background in agricultural management, Gorbachev was no more able or willing to adopt radical solutions to the land. In late 1988, he proposed leasing land to individuals and families. Although the land would still be state-owned (the conservatives would not sanction outright privatization, and Gorbachev himself was not prepared to go so far), the lessees would have title for 50 years and the right to sell most of their produce on the open market. Here, too, the opposition of regional Party officials managed to block most reform. Given the power they had in their local districts, they could make life very difficult for entrepreneurial peasants. Besides, many prospective free farmers could see little point in developing farms the state could snatch back at any time. As with political reform, Gorbachev would find it easier to undermine the existing system than reform or replace it. The existing 'command-administrative' economic system was weakened enough to be even less efficient, but not enough that market economics could begin to operate.

Rolling Back the Empire

Gorbachev was, by contrast, far more successful in developing his new brand of Soviet foreign policy. By his summit meeting with US President Reagan in Moscow in May 1988, he would have stamped his authority on the Defence Ministry, publicly abandoned the 'Brezhnev Doctrine' whereby the USSR reserved the right to invade any of its client states if it felt its interests threatened and even reached an agreement on the withdrawal of Soviet troops from Afghanistan. This last was a particular triumph, as he came to office already convinced that withdrawal was inevitable. At the XXVII Party Congress, Gorbachev publicly admitted that the Afghan war, then in its sixth year and with no victory in sight, was another disastrous mistake. It was, he said, 'a bleeding wound', and one which he committed himself to staunching.

Withdrawal (which took place in late 1988 and early 1989) did not just require the conclusion of a satisfyingly face-saving treaty with the rebels and their US backers, though. It also reflected the culmination of a behind-the-scenes campaign to force the security establishment to accept that the days of Soviet global imperialism were over. His best opportunity to tighten his grip upon the military came in May 1987, when the young German pilot Matthias Rust flew across the Soviet border and landed in Red Square. While the episode had much of the farcical about it, Rust could as easily have been a terrorist or a spy, and this humiliating failure of the Soviet air defence network gave Gorbachev the perfect opportunity to flash those 'iron teeth' of his again. Defence Minister Sokolov and a collection of other conservative military leaders were sacked. For Sokolov's replacement, Gorbachev turned not to the obvious ministry insiders but the relatively junior General Dmitri Yazov. A training specialist formerly from the Central Asian and Far Eastern Military Districts, Yazov seemed relatively aware of the need for reform but above all he was an outsider. To Gorbachev, he seemed sensible but also politically weak, and the General Secretary wanted a minister he felt he could control.

In due course, Yazov would become a liability rather than an asset, but for the moment his appointment gave Gorbachev a much freer hand to redefine Soviet security policy and try to clinch arms reduction deals with the USA. At the Washington Summit in December 1987, he clinched the INF (Intermediate-range Nuclear Forces) treaty which limited medium-range weapons, while the agreement on a withdrawal from Afghanistan, concluded in February 1988, opened the way for a new round of regional accords. This determination to cut deals says much about Gorbachev's character and his position. The USSR could not afford its existing nuclear arsenal, much less to modernize it. In an era of precision-guided missiles and guerrilla wars, its huge army of tanks and mechanized infantry was increasingly an expensive anachronism. The military and the nationalist wing of the Party would not yet tolerate major unilateral cuts, though, and so Gorbachev had to have something to show them that he was not making the USSR vulnerable. After all, the experience of Nazi invasion in the Second World War had left many of the older generation almost paranoid in their desire to scc the USSR militarily secure. Beyond this, Gorbachev was by nature a man to play his every card as cannily as possible. If he had to cut his armed forces, then he would still try to use them to win concessions from the USA and a global reputation as a peacemaker.

Opposition to Gorbachev: Conservatives

Gorbachev needed his political skills, as he was to face mounting opposition from conservatives within the Party and from radicals both within the Party and outside it. Behind the closed doors of the January 1987 Plenum of the Central Committee, Gorbachev had accused the Party of resisting reform. He was right, but this was less the product of a deliberate conspiracy and more to do with the conservative habits of so many within it and also the lack of a clear and coherent policy for change. Given that Gorbachev was still trying to come to grips with the problems facing the USSR and hopping from one possible reform to the next, it was hardly surprising that few within the Party could or wanted to keep up with him. I remember a later conversation with a retired Party official, in which he remembered 1987 as a year of 'rollercoaster reform, but only in Gorbachev's head'.

This was unfair, but reflected the mood of many within the *apparat*. The more radical Gorbachev's solutions and the less cautious his tactics, the more conservatives would actively resist. In December 1986, for example, he dismissed Dinmukhamed Kunayev, Party First Secretary for Kazakhstan. A close friend of Brezhnev's, Kunayev had presided over massive corruption in his republic. When Gorbachev announced that he would be replaced by Gennadi Kolbin, an ally of his and a Russian at that, the Kazakh elite united in resistance as it was clear that Kolbin was being appointed with a mandate to clean up the rest of the republic. They could not resist Gorbachev openly within the Party, so they instead whipped up protests in the republic's capital, Alma-Ata. Traditional anti-Russian feelings were encouraged, the police instructed to hold back from dispersing the crowds, and local strongmen who had done well under Kunayev bussed in their supporters to swell the mob. In the event, none of this stopped Kolbin from being appointed, though he found it difficult to make much headway when the whole republican elite was united in obstruction to his anti-corruption campaign, but it showed how conservatives were beginning to consider using violence and local politics to resist reform.

Others, though, had rather more creditable reasons for becoming wary of Gorbachev. Rather than strengthening the USSR, he seemed to be weakening it, trading away its nuclear defences and introducing a hotchpotch of ill-considered economic reforms which led to a fall in economic growth from 4 per cent in 1986 to 1.3 per cent in 1987. As Gorbachev shifted ground, he inevitably left behind even some of his erstwhile allies, a process best illustrated by Yegor Ligachev, the Siberian Party boss whom Andropov brought into the Central Committee and Gorbachev made his virtual second-in-command in 1985. Despite subsequent attempts to smear him, Ligachev was no corrupt and self-serving relic of the Brezhnev era but an intelligent man of puritanical instincts and strong principles. Ligachev is usually described as a 'conservative', but this is too simplistic. He had been a wholehearted supporter of the early, Andropovian style of reform: *uskoreniye*, the campaign against alcoholism, the crack-down on corruption within the Party. One of the few politicians who did not change his principles during the six hectic years of the Gorbachev era, he was increasingly to feel that it was the General Secretary who had betrayed Andropov and the type of reform for which he stood. Although there is no evidence that he ever sought such a position, Ligachev increasingly became the symbol of a new breed of conservatives, men who rejected Brezhnevism but who also felt Gorbachev was going too far.

In December 1987, Gorbachev admitted that he faced 'a certain intensification of resistance by conservative forces', although 'naturally these people never say that they oppose *perestroika* [only] ... its negative side-effects'. For the moment, though, their resistance was largely passive. In presenting the plan for 1988, for example, the Chair of *Gosplan*, Nikolai Talyzin, simply ignored new guidelines intended to introduce new flexibility for factory managers. Eventually the huge *Uralmash* combine challenged him and won (not least because Prime Minister Ryzhkov had previously run the enterprise). Talyzin was in the meantime sacked, but for every such piece of passive resistance exposed, more succeeded. The more open threat, though, came from radicals who felt Gorbachev was not going far enough.

Opposition to Gorbachev: Radicals

The radicals, too, acquired their figurehead: Boris Yeltsin. Like Ligachev, he had at one stage been seen as one of Gorbachev's team. Formerly Party Secretary of the industrial city of Sverdlovsk, Yeltsin had been appointed on to the Central Committee in June 1985, a beneficiary of the initial purge of the *apparat*. In December, he was made Party Secretary of Moscow. This was not only a powerful job, it was a very sensitive one. Yeltsin threw himself into his job with enthusiasm, above all launching a populist campaign against bureaucracy and privilege and the most extensive purge of the city's civil service since the Stalin era. Like Gorbachev, he went on walkabouts to establish his credentials as a man of the people and even took a few well publicized trips on public transport (even though he soon returned to the security and comfort of his official limousine). Yeltsin trod on too many toes and found himself the subject of a whispering campaign in the Kremlin, in part orchestrated by Ligachev, who saw him as a dangerously erratic and destructive maverick. Characteristically impulsive and combative, Yeltsin took the offensive. In September 1987 he wrote a personal letter to Gorbachev in which he complained that 'there has practically been no *perestroika* at all', only 'a lot of inflated language for public consumption, while in reality the implementation has been pettifogging, self-serving and bureaucratic'. Much of the blame he laid on Ligachev. Next month, at another Central Committee Plenum, he unleashed an even more savage onslaught, in which he also criticized Gorbachev and tendered his resignation from the Politburo and from his job in Moscow.

Until this point, Yeltsin had been useful to Gorbachev. His natural desire to place himself at the middle of political disputes and play extremes against each other meant that Yeltsin was a handy counter-weight to Ligachev and other hard-liners. Yet once Yeltsin also began criticizing him and did so in a way and language at odds with the usual etiquette of Party disputes, he became a liability. Gorbachev allowed Ligachev and others to humiliate their rival, and in February 1988, Yeltsin was dragged from his hospital bed, where he was recovering from illness, and formally dropped from the Politburo. It was a spectacle of vindictiveness from which no one emerged with much credit, but what became called the 'Yeltsin Affair' was significant for a number of reasons. It brought divisions within the Party into the open and it established Yeltsin's credentials as a popular figure around whom growing resistance to the CPSU and its grip on society could unite.

This was important precisely because reform was beginning to liberate forces Gorbachev would fail to understand, much less control. Chief of these was nationalism. As the Kunayev incident had shown, anti-Russian feelings may have been suppressed for decades but were still strong, they were the product both of the imposition of Russian language and culture as a result of tsarist and then Soviet imperial control and the practical implications of being very much second-class citizens in a Russian-dominated state. Russians represented just over 50 per cent of the total population, but even they were not necessarily supporters of imperial rule. This was, after all, a very peculiar empire, in which the dominant group was not a race but a political class largely comprising Russians and other Slavs. Most Russians had not benefited from Moscow's control over other peoples; quite the opposite, as many of the non-Russian republics received more subsidies than they provided the treasury. In addition, though, nationalist tensions re-emerged between subject peoples. Armenia and Azerbaijan had a long-standing dispute over the Nagorno-Karabakh Autonomous Oblast, an enclave of Christian Armenians within Moslem Azerbaijan. In February 1988, demonstrations in Armenia called for the transfer of the region to Armenian control. In response, Azeris in the town of Sumgait rioted, killing more than 30 Armenians.

Glasnost' invited greater political participation from the people. As such, it was another step in Gorbachev's faltering path towards democratization. He was never quite able to see the people as a more natural constituency for him than the Party. He still demonstrated genuine if, with hindsight, naive belief in their commitment to his vision of a revived Party and USSR. Yet it also liberated many pressures and passions, from the masses' resentment of the privileges of the elite to a new interest in religion. At the XIX Party Conference in June 1988, Gorbachev was to outline a dramatic programme intended to harness these energies behind reform, including contested elections and a limit on the Party's ability to control access to key jobs. He had conclusively outgrown Andropov's type of reform, but was on the verge of his greatest gamble yet.

Reading and Sources

The one obvious source, Gorbachev's own *Perestroika*, is perhaps the least useful. It is at least worth looking at to get an idea of just how roundabout and unclear his thought processes really were. Then move on to sharper analytical studies, discussed in the Bibliography, or the writings of some of those about him. Ligachev's memoirs, *Inside Gorbachev's Kremlin*, provide some useful insights, while Alexander Dallinn and Gail Lapidus have edited an excellent collection of Soviet and Western writings together as *The Soviet System in Crisis*.

An effective survey of the catastrophe at Chernobyl' is David Marples' book *Chernobyl and Nuclear Power in the USSR* (1987, Macmillan). My own book *Afghanistan: The Soviet Union's Last War* (1995, Frank Cass) not only summarizes my research about the decision to withdraw, but also uses the war to illustrate both the workings of *glasnost'* and the rise of the informal movement. A useful study of the *neformaly* and the way they proved the foundation for an increasingly pluralist form of politics is *The Road to Post-Communism*, edited by Geoffrey Hosking, Peter Duncan and Jonathan Aves (1992, Pinter). The liberation of literature and journalism is nicely discussed in David Wedgewood Benn's *From Glasnost to Freedom of Speech* (1992, Pinter) and Alec Nove's *Glasnost in Action* (1990, Unwin Hyman), while the anthology *Glasnost'*, edited by Helena Goscilo and Byron Lindsay (1990, Ardis) collects together a variety of the writings of the time. Anders Aslund's *Gorbachev's Struggle for Economic Reform* and David Dyker's *Restructuring the Soviet Economy* (1992, Routledge), by contrast, are rather more sober assessments of the economic problems of the time.

6

GORBACHEV THE GAMBLER: DEMOCRATIZATION

During his early days in office, the time of *uskoreniye*, Gorbachev had assumed that the main obstacle to meaningful reform would be the laziness and self-interest of individual scoundrels and slackers, and so he tried to purge them and spur them on. Later he turned to *glasnost'* when he began to see the problem more in terms of the need to mobilize opinion and isolate enemies of reform within the Party. Increasingly, though, he came to see the problem not to be particular people within the CPSU so much as the institution of the Party itself. Some urged him then to break with it, but Gorbachev's problem was that he was trying to reconcile his divided loyalties. He was a genuinely committed Communist and also a Soviet/Russian patriot. The one required him to stay within the Party and reform it from within, the other to break the Party and thus its dead grip upon the country.

Gorbachev was never one to aim low, and thus he chose to try and do both. Desperate to find some tool with which to force the CPSU to reform itself, he moved to introduce some form of democracy to the USSR, an audacious and ultimately disastrous gamble. From this point, between his decision in mid-1988 to call national elections to a new parliament and his election in March 1990 to the newly developed position of Soviet President, he became overtaken by events. He proved able to break the power and the morale of the old Party–State system, but failed to create anything in its place.

Why *Perestroika* was not Working

The USSR and Russia had never known democracy. Following defeat in the 1904–5 Russo-Japanese War, a series of local uprisings rather inaccurately known as the '1905 Revolution' had forced Tsar Nicholas II to hold elections to Russia's first parliament, or *Duma*. The voting system excluded women and an increasing proportion of poorer men, and was structured to squeeze out more radical parties. Even so, the first *Duma* tried to assert its authority. In response, the Tsar dissolved it and held new elections on an even more restricted franchise. When this new *Duma* again proved not to be to his liking, Nicholas repeated the whole process until he had a properly subservient parliament. Similarly, attempts during the early years of the Bolshevik regime to democratize the USSR were soon abandoned, in part because fighting the 1919–21 Civil War required a strong, centralized command system and in part because Lenin and his allies thought founding democracy should take second place to building socialism. Gorbachev was thus taking a bold and dramatic step into the unknown. Yet one of Gorbachev's virtues was a willingness to admit failure but not defeat: to realize that one approach was not working and not give up hope but seek another way to his goal. By mid- to late 1988, there was ample evidence that *perestroika* was not working. Instead, the country seemed to be nearing an economic, social and political crisis.

As discussed in Chapter 5, Gorbachev's economic strategy had been counter-productive and ruinous. He had tried to allow greater individual enterprise through the co-operative movement and increased autonomy for local management, but without taking away the pressure for instant results which meant that no one had any breathing space in which to introduce new ideas or technology. He cut back on the central bureaucracy which had previously co-ordinated the economy, but without creating the sort of national market which could take its place. He wanted high technology industry, but with the budget deficit running at 35 billion rubles, he could not afford to pay for new plant or training. He told the bureaucracy to reform the economy, but he had no clear blueprint for such reform and failed to convince them that such reforms were good either for themselves or the country. He demanded that the workers work harder, but without either the carrots to induce them to do so or the sticks which could enforce it.

This reflected Gorbachev's own lack of mastery of economics. Many Western leaders find it hard enough to manage an economy, even with teams of skilled and experienced advisers. Gorbachev, by contrast, was the product of a political system which had for decades ignored the realities of economic theory and actively discouraged its objective study. In addition, this was an issue over which the leadership was sharply divided. Increasingly Gorbachev, Shevardnadze and Yakovlev took up a relatively radical position, whereas Ligachev continued to resist it. He felt that a new emphasis on private property (and thus some enriching themselves at the expense of the rest) went against the ideals of the Party. In the middle, Prime Minister Ryzhkov, himself a former manager, argued the case for a more cautious compromise, which would rationalize but still retain central planning and state control of the economy.

As a result, there was a lack of any clear direction to economic reform. Instead, a series of short-sighted and often contradictory measures only continued to worsen matters. The failure of the economic side to *perestroika* inevitably had implications for the social aspects of reform. By the beginning of 1988, it was becoming clear to Gorbachev and his closest allies that they could not expect any imminent improvement in the economy. In fact, it was to prove on the verge of complete collapse. This was both a cause and an effect of their political problems. So long as reform seemed to be failing, then their position within the leadership only deteriorated. Without a strong mandate for change, though, they could never bring about the sort of dramatic reforms which might have a chance of saving the USSR. This was another pivotal moment in Gorbachev's era, and one in which he took another important step away from his earlier, limited notions of reform towards a genuine revolution in Soviet politics.

Gorbachev's Solution: Democratization

For Gorbachev's solution was *demokratizatsiya*, 'democratization'. By this he did not mean a full and immediate transition
to a Western-style system, with rival parties, changes of governments and fully open, free and fair elections. But he did mean
trying to introduce an unprecedented level of mass political
participation into the system. While 'democratizaton' was not
intended to challenge the CPSU's control of the USSR, it
would mean more aspects of daily life would be freed from
ideological control, and there would greater opportunity to
influence Party policy. Radicals had been trying to convince
him of the need for democratization for some time, and he
himself had clearly been toying with the idea. He had first
introduced the notion of 'pluralism', of an acceptance of
different points of view in July 1987, while in February 1987 he
had said that the only choice was 'either democracy or social
inertia and conservatism'. Gorbachev was forever introducing
reformist notions and then letting them disappear from view,
though, and introducing pluralism into a system which for so
long had been built on rigid Party discipline, on the vigorous
suppression of rival or unorthodox views, was bound to be both
dangerous and contentious. What finally convinced him that he
needed to take this dramatic step?

First of all, it went with the grain of many of his own views
and instincts. Trained as a lawyer, he could see the advantages
of creating an institutional foundation to reform. After all, up
to then he had introduced new policies, not changed the way
those policies were made. A new General Secretary could
reverse these reforms with ease. In other words, he had introduced innovative policies, but without reforming the underlying political machine. Another of Gorbachev's catchphrases,
and one in which he probably really believed, was the notion of
the 'law-governed state'. The old ways had been marked by
laws no one obeyed – least of all the elite – but Gorbachev
hoped that new laws, made and upheld by a new legislative
body, could at last make the USSR that 'law-governed state'.

There were also pragmatic political reasons for taking this
step at this time. Gorbachev could not afford to ignore the fact

that his relations with the Party and the people alike were worsening. Democratization thus represented 'shock therapy' for the Party, an attempt to force the *apparatchiki* to accept the need for change. It would demonstrate the extent of the public groundswell in support of it and place limits on the power of an elite he could no longer trust. At the same time, Gorbachev hoped that by giving the ordinary citizen some say in the governance of the state, he could also create some new legitimacy for the Party's rule. In this way, Gorbachev meant to create a Party both more in line with his own ideas and at the same time with a renewed popular mandate. In his calculations, at worse it would at least leave a more permanent and formal reformist legacy to the USSR and undermine the power of many of his rivals within the Party. In fact, it would prove far more dangerous to his dreams of a revived CPSU and USSR than he had dreamt.

The third and final imperative behind democratization was linked with one of the general considerations behind *glasnost'*. The USSR had not only run low on money and on morale, it had run low on inspiration. Politics is about argument and opinion, about developing, debating and defending rival points of view. In other words, it is about ideas. Decades of ideological conformity had diminished Soviet society's capacity to develop new ideas, and that which was left was all too often stilted and stunted. It had bred a nation of managers, problem-solvers able to respond to orders and situations, whether hungry citizens working their way round the bureaucracy to get the food they needed or sober bureaucrats applying the latest Party line. But the Party had excluded and alienated most of the people who could go beyond responding to circumstance and actually devise forward-looking strategies for change. A running theme through *glasnost'*, through Gorbachev's eagerness for contacts with the West and now with democratization was the need to free Soviet society from the mental straitjackets of the past.

Demokratizatsiya was thus a necessary extension to *glasnost'* and the extension of popular participation represented by the *neformaly*. Yet it also carried formidable dangers. The real threat was something Gorbachev had not predicted, that far from being able to control and use this process, he would instead be increasingly at its mercy. At this time, Gorbachev was fixated by the threat posed by conservatives within the Party, and he knew democratization would be seen by them as a further betrayal of the CPSU. What is more, they were right. Elections previously had been stage-managed, with a single – Party – candidate. Everyone was expected to participate in what was not an expression of popular sovereignty so much as a public act of homage to the state. By giving the people some real power – however limited this might be at first – Gorbachev was introducing the dangerous notion that political legitimacy was vested not in the Party's self-proclaimed mission to lead the Soviet people to Communism but a public vote of support that could as easily be lost.

The XIX Party Conference

Aware of the potential for resistance, Gorbachev chose to launch his latest brainchild at the XIX Party Conference in June–July 1988. He prepared the ground with some care, dropping broad hints that new changes were in the air as early as a plenary meeting of the Central Committee in February, where he warned that there would be 'no half measures'. At the same time, he moved to shore up his vulnerable right flank by taking a much stronger line with his conservative critics. In March, the hard-line newspaper *Sovetskaya Rossiya* published an open letter from a Leningrad school teacher named Nina Andreyeva which represented a clear challenge to the reformists. Headed 'I Cannot Betray My Principles', it was a Stalinist tract full of Russian nationalist sentiment and it implicitly accused Gorbachev of betraying Marxism–Leninism. Such an overt attack on the leadership was unheard of in the mainstream press, and cannot but have had at least encouragement from Ligachev and other highly placed sceptics. He certainly did his best to capitalize on the letter's impact. As usual, though, a direct threat burnt away Gorbachev's habitual caution. He responded with a combative reassertion of his position, while *Pravda* carried a heavyweight rejection of the letter apparently drafted by Alexander Yakovlev himself. The editor of *Sovetskaya Rossiya* was forced into a public apology for publishing the letter. Ligachev had enough supporters within the Central Committee to prevent Gorbachev from sacking him just yet, but relations between the two were at best frosty and several of Ligachev's clients and allies were sacked or demoted on various pretexts.

The XIX Party Conference was clearly going to be a pivotal moment for *perestroika*, and was marked by almost unprecedentedly sharp disagreements between different wings and factions of the Party. Since Stalin's purges of the late 1920s, conferences had never been the site of such open resistance to the leadership. Boris Yeltsin and Yegor Ligachev, standard-bearers of the radical and conservative wings respectively, clashed openly. Ministers and bureaucrats revealed hitherto secret information on the state of the USSR, from Health Minister Chazov's admission that life expectancy had slipped to 32nd in the world to the news that half the country's schools lacked running water or central heating. Amidst this storm of political wheeling and dealing, Gorbachev was in his element. Yeltsin and Ligachev he played off against one another, again presenting himself as the moderate of the centre and again using the radicals to raise issues and make accusations he felt he could not do himself.

Above all, though, the Conference was dominated by Gorbachev's proposals for a new parliamentary system to institutionalize *demokratizatsiya*. He envisaged replacing the existing powerless parliament with a new two-chamber Supreme Soviet with 450 deputies (this would later rise to 542). These members, in turn, would be elected from a much larger chamber, the 2000-strong Congress of People's Deputies (later expanded to 2250). This Congress would be the country's highest legislative body, but as it would only meet once a year (except for emergency sessions), it would largely confine itself to electing the members of the Supreme Soviet and ratifying its actions (see Figure 3). With such a working parliament in place, Gorbachev furthermore argued that there had to be a much sharper line drawn between the Party and the state. In other words, while he was certainly not suggesting that the Party should no longer guide the governance of the USSR – this was, after all, still written in as Article Six of the constitution – he wanted to untangle the roles of the Party and the state. In this he was acually reviving one of Lenin's concerns, that the Party should determine the country's general course, yet not merge to form a cosy, all-embracing ruling elite with the state bureaucracy, which should be free to turn these guidelines into specific policies. Gorbachev himself would have two roles, both as General Secretary of the CPSU and also as Chair of the Supreme Soviet (and thus head of state, or President). This not only gave him some power base independent of the Party, it issued a challenge to regional Party bosses. In the past, they had automatically also been members of the Supreme Soviet as well as their local Soviets. Henceforth, if they also wanted to have a direct say in the new politics, they would have to be elected.

The proposals were passed, even though many had their reservations. The most radical Party delegates were concerned Gorbachev had not gone far enough. The conservatives, who might have been expected to be more critical, were on the whole silent. In part, they were relieved Gorbachev had not gone too far, but on the whole they were reassured by his efforts to safeguard the position of the Party. His rhetoric, after all, underlined this ambiguity in his position. On the one hand, he proclaimed that '*Glasnost*' means pluralism of opinion on any issues of domestic and foreign policy, free collation of different points of view, debates.' On the other, though, he warned against such 'abuses of democratization' as setting up other parties to rival the CPSU, something 'fundamentally against the needs of *perestroika*'. It was difficult to avoid the conclusion that Gorbachev wanted people to have different ideas, but be prepared to wait for the Party to do anything about them.

Both because he wanted the CPSU to continue to exercise its leading role and also because he knew he had to placate the conservative majority, Gorbachev built into his new system what became known as 'anti-democratic filters'. These served to satisfy the conservatives, but meant that *demokratizatsiya* failed, and only served further to undermine Gorbachev's reformist campaign. First of all, local Party structures would play a large role in the elections, using everything from propaganda to dirty tricks to swing the vote. In particular, they dominated local electoral commissions which so often blatantly excluded anti-Party candidates from the running that these bodies were actually abolished in 1989. Secondly, 750 seats in the Congress were reserved for representatives of public bodies ranging from the CPSU itself (which was given 100 seats) to the Soviet temperance society (which received one). Most of these were by definition controlled by the Party, meaning that it already had direct control over a third of the Congress, even without winning a single election. Thirdly, the two-tier system encouraged and allowed the Party to rig the membership of the Supreme Soviet, in which real power rested. The two-tier approach made sense in that it allowed the creation of a parliament small enough to work, but without making constituencies too huge to make sense (if the Supreme Soviet had been directly elected, an average constituency would have been twice the size of Wales). But it also meant that whoever could assemble a working majority in the Congress of People's Deputies – and the Party had already awarded itself a third of the votes – could play a disproportionate part in deciding the membership of the Supreme Soviet. In this Gorbachev the politician triumphed over Gorbachev the reformer. In order to keep the conservatives from open rebellion, he built so many contradictions and compromises into his new system that it would destroy, not save, the USSR.

This is the verdict of hindsight, though. It was still a bold and dramatic move, and it caught the imagination of a Soviet people who had otherwise become jaded by empty talk of reform. The elections were set for March 1989, with the Congress of People's Deputies meeting in April. In many ways, the next year was dominated by these dates, as a system struggled to adjust to new political rules. In the centre, Gorbachev presided over a further easing of Cold War tensions, described below, as well as a new round of personnel reshuffles. Above all, Gorbachev increasingly sought to marginalize Ligachev, both by reforming the Party Secretariat and handing him the agriculture portfolio, ironically enough the very job Gorbachev had first held when he came to Moscow in 1978. Furthermore, Gorbachev tried to shore up his position by appointing new heads to the KGB and the Interior Ministry

(MVD). The KGB went to Vladimir Kryuchkov, formerly the service's chief of foreign intelligence. As another protégé of Andropov's, Gorbachev hoped that his respect for his patron and his awareness of the international scene would ensure Kryuchkov's loyalty. In this he would ultimately be mistaken, as Kryuchkov was one of the prime movers behind the 1991 coup. The MVD went to Vadim Bakatin, a long-time associate of Gorbachev's.

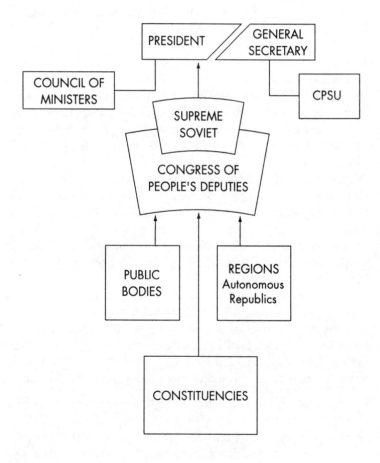

Figure 3: The Reformed System of Government in the USSR

Politics Comes to the Soviet Union

The dominant issue of the moment was the rise of the 'new politics', as Party and outsiders alike tried to adapt. This proved to be a truly catalytic event, and shaped the last years of the USSR.

- It created a wave of public optimism, as hopes were raised which would almost inevitably be dashed. Gorbachev's renewed popularity would prove short-lived, and any further promises of change treated with extreme suspicion.
- It led to the rise of a whole new generation of politicians outside the Party, especially anti-Party nationalists such as Boris Yeltsin. Gorbachev had the chance to turn these into a new cohort of allies, but he never took it. In part, at least, this reflected his naturally imperious style: as has often been said, he wanted supporters, not colleagues. These new politicians were either not prepared to be treated as subordinates or could not afford to lose face in front of their electorates.
- It galvanized resistance to Gorbachev and his central power base from every quarter. By creating a system dominated by the Party (and conservatives within it, at that), *demokratizatsiya* forced these newcomers to move into open opposition if they were to have any political life or success at all. At the same time, either humiliated by the elections or forced to campaign on local issues, the conservatives and the local Party bosses increasingly saw their only chance at political survival in opposing Moscow and reform.
- Finally, and in part as a result of the last points, the new structure failed to take into account the growing need and demand for a decentralization of power. As a result, it only strengthened local nationalisms and resistance to the centre.

From personal experience, I can attest to the uplifting and often worrying enthusiasm of many of these campaigners. Uplifting, because of the optimism and energy liberated by the prospect of democratization. Campaigners denied access to print shops and photocopiers by the local Party, for example, would resort to copying out election fliers by hand, painstakingly writing out the same slogans and promises again and again. When the Congress actually met, it was televised for a few days and everyone watched, rapt by the unprecedented sight of Soviet politicians holding different views and actually arguing them in public. Live transmissions had to be suspended as labour productivity fell by around a fifth: people watched TV or radio rather than work. Worrying, because the optimism and enthusiasm were often so sharply out of line with the realities of the situation. This was not full democracy, and the Party was bound to squeeze out most rival candidates. Similarly, too many people expected prompt and very practical gains from the elections, ranging from access to hitherto scarce consumer goods to fairer pay scales. A poor country such as the USSR could not hope to meet these expectations, any more than the existing elite were likely to give up their power and perks following a mere election.

Between December 1988 and the end of February 1989, the battle was to get on the ballot papers for the elections. The nomination process was clumsy, probably deliberately so, as it allowed Party-dominated registration committees extra scope to exclude opposition candidates. Better-known figures such as Boris Yeltsin and the former dissident Andrei Sakharov were able to get through such organized filibustering, thanks to their public profile. Although 60 scientific organizations had nominated him for one of the Academy of Science's list candidates, its conservative leadership tried to exclude Sakharov until forced to reconsider by a storm of protest within its ranks. Having been sentenced to internal exile in the city of Gorki for his criticism of the invasion of Afghanistan, he had been released at Gorbachev's initiative in 1986. One of the USSR's most celebrated scientists, three times Hero of the Soviet Union and a winner of the Nobel Peace Prize, Sakharov represented a tradition of democratic liberalism and a personal integrity which made him a leading light of the reformist movement until his death in 1989. As this shows, the new generation of opposition political figures who rose during the campaign had to have some strong basis on which to challenge the *apparat*. For some, like the Olympic weightlifter Yuri Vlasov and the poet Yevgeni Yevtushenko, it was their fame. Others won notoriety by the very vehemence and extremism of their rhetoric or their role as embodiments of resistance to the Party. This was especially true of Boris Yeltsin. Having failed to win political rehabilitation at the XIX Party Conference, Boris Yeltsin further distanced himself from the CPSU. In an open challenge, his March 1989 election manifesto called for a 'struggle against the existing elitist bureaucratic stratum', land reform and the subordination of the Party both to parliament and the law. In February 1989 he went even further, suggesting that there was scope for a multi-party system in the USSR – a dramatic statement for one still officially a member of the CPSU. In many cases, especially outside Russia, candidates made it on to the ballot form by championing local interests for, as will be discussed below, the elections proved a catalyst of nationalisms of every kind.

In many ways, Sakharov and Yeltsin were the two founding fathers of the anti-Party democratic movement, and despite the clear respect the ex-*apparatchik* held for the scientist, the two could be said to represent its two wings. Sakharov was heir to a Westwards-looking tradition, which sought to bring a European and North American political culture to Russia. Transparent and accountable democratic politics, a plurality of political views, a law which applied equally to all – these were the bases of his vision of a future society. Yeltsin's democratism, though, was a much more traditionally Russian phenomenon, rooted in centuries of absolutism and his own background as a prefect of the Party, as witnessed by the increasing authoritarianism of his post-Soviet regime. For the moment, though, the democratic movement appreciated that it had to stay united. Even though it contained many who were still members of the Party – Yeltsin himself only resigned in 1990 – one of the issues around which the democratic movement could and had to unite was opposition to the slow and limited nature of Gorbachev's reforms. Yeltsin's campaign had been based around his judgement that *perestroika* had been badly thought-out and implemented far too slowly. His calls for greater democracy and an end to the power and privileges of the Party and bureaucracy were general slogans rather than detailed plans for the future. Yet they staked out his stand against the

CPSU leadership and won wide support among the intelligentsia and workers alike. He polled the single largest popular mandate of the elections, defeating his Party-backed rival with 89 per cent of the vote.

Relations between Gorbachev and the Party were even more complex, but equally fraught. In March 1989, a Plenum of the Central Committee voted on who would get the Party's 100 guaranteed seats in the Congress of People's Deputies. The results showed that no one faction was dominant. While Gorbachev was duly elected, so too were both Yegor Ligachev and his radical sparring partner Alexander Yakovlev. In the actual elections proper, though, Party bosses and conservatives in particular polled very badly. Thirty-four regional Party Secretaries were defeated, while overall one in five Communist officials standing lost, despite the backing of the CPSU machine.

In the Congress as a whole, Communists had 87 per cent of the seats. The more detailed electoral arithmetic, though, was more alarming for them. It may seem a strong showing, but the Party already dominated the organizations given 33 per cent of the seats, and in 27 per cent of constituencies it had managed to prevent the registration of any rival to its own candidate. Those opposition candidates who were elected tended to be the most outspoken and radical. Under Boris Yeltsin, they banded together to form the Inter-Regional Group of Deputies in July. While numbering no more than a fifth of the deputies to Congress, this was still a legal and open opposition grouping to the CPSU: something not seen for 65 years. More ominously, in the Baltic states, broad nationalist groupings calling themselves Popular Fronts routed the communists. Their victory in these and local elections were to make a mockery of the Party's 'leading role', and contributed to the decision to remove Article Six from the constitution in 1990.

In the subsequent elections within the Congress to the Supreme Soviet, the Party ensured that it secured the majority of seats, even if it could not prevent many of the most vocal and popular radicals from also making it on to the country's standing parliament, including Sakharov and Yeltsin. This was by no means a triumph for Gorbachev, though. Although he was duly elected Chair of the Supreme Soviet, he found himself unable to use this new post as he had expected. The Party majority was largely made up of opponents of his reforms, while the radicals depended on their strong anti-Party stance for their position and thus could not afford to cut deals with him. Gorbachev had an opportunity to move away from the Party but, as will be discussed later, he felt he could not do so. There were great expectations for this new legislature, but it was bitterly divided and there was no clear idea of just what it was meant to do. The election of a semi-democratic parliament, after all, was not accompanied by any reform of the bureaucracy. Instead, the new parliament and the Inter-Regional Group of Deputies represented new foci for agitation and the election had shown the depth of popular dissatisfaction. This was especially true in regions such as the Baltic states and Transcaucasia, where nationalism was a rising force.

The End of Empire

Nationalist tensions had long been present within the USSR, albeit strictly controlled. Tsarist and Soviet history was full of injustices done by the state to constituent peoples, from the legacy of imperial control in Central Asia and Transcaucasia through to Stalin's policy of mass deportations. The entire Chechen people of southern Russia were deported in one night in 1944, scattered in Siberia and Central Asia in an operation which left 200 000 dead, more than one in five. Similar treatment had been meted out to the Crimean Tatars, who were one of the first peoples to use the new freedoms of *glasnost'* to press their claims for justice. Among the early informal movements were groups committed to championing national rights. In some cases these were Russian nationalists who, for example, devoted themselves to restoring tsarist monuments. Often, though, they instead agitated on behalf of minority rights, such as those of the Tatars, or the Balts, or the Armenians of Nagorno-Karabakh.

In due course, these *neformaly* became the kernels of nationalist movements which would take an increasingly strong line in asserting their interests and which would both use and be transformed by democratization. In part this was a grassroots phenomenon. Citizens became increasingly conscious of their national – as opposed to Soviet – identity and looked to form and support movements espousing them. In the Baltic states, for example, the Popular Fronts rose precisely as such expressions of anti-imperial, anti-Soviet, anti-Party and anti-Russian sentiment. Elsewhere, though, nationalism was encouraged and harnessed by members of the existing elite. It had already become clear that local elites could and would play the nationalist card against Moscow when they felt threatened. This had been shown in 1986 when the Kazakh Party had resisted the appointment of an outsider, and it would become increasingly common in an age when formerly unassailable members of the *apparat* suddenly had to face election. Although there was as yet no direct link between electoral success and position within the government, that was the implication of holding elections in the first place. The Leningrad Party apparatus had been especially unsuccessful in the elections to the Congress, for example, and in July 1989 it met in Gorbachev's presence to sack its incumbent leader and replace him with Boris Gidaspov, one of the few local *apparatchiki* who had won in the elections. The message was clear: adapt to the new rules of *demokratizatsiya* or fall by the wayside

The local elites adapted and developed for themselves new power bases, but not as Gorbachev had expected. In many cases, where once they had based their position on their role as the local agents of Moscow, instead they moved to establish themselves as the voices of local resistance to Moscow. Radical nationalists who lacked the elites' political machine and network of contacts often found themselves forced back into the political margins or co-opted into these new nationalist forces. In Lithuania, for example, Party First Secretary Algirdas Brazauskas responded to the rise of the Popular Front by adopting an increasingly strong line on the need to champion local interests. The case of Brazaskaus is an interesting and in many ways typical one. As an ally, he and similar flexible local Communists would have been invaluable. Yet instead of building bridges, Gorbachev bullied and berated him and turned a potential loyalist into a critic and rival. In December

1989, the Lithuanian Communist Party formally split from the CPSU and set itself up as a separate social democratic party. In the short term, it failed to stem the nationalist advance, but in 1992, this new 'Lithuanian Democratic Labour Party' was to surge back to power on the back of a decisive popular vote.

Most striking of all, though, were developments in Transcaucasia. In Georgia, the Party at first tried to face down the nationalists. In April 1989, Gorbachev's absence on a trip abroad became the pretext for a show of force by hard-liners both locally and in Moscow. This led to a massacre in the capital, Tbilisi, when paratroopers and security troops dispersed a crowd of protesters with riot gas, truncheons and entrenching tools, killing 20. This galvanized Georgian nationalism, and even forced Foreign Minister Shevardnadze – a former Georgian Party Secretary – to distance himself from the leadership. By August 1989, public protests and boycotts had forced the local authorities to hold multi-party elections. The result was the first non-Communist republican parliament in the USSR and the rise of the militant nationalist leader Zviad Gamsakhurdia. He would go on to declare Georgian independence in April 1991. In Azerbaijan and Armenia, the local Parties went even further, each swinging behind nationalist militants over the issue of Nagorno-Karabakh, a contested region populated by Armenians under Azeri control. By January 1990, local banditry and terrorism had escalated to effective guerrilla war. Following an outburst of rioting in the Azeri capital, Baku, Russian troops had to be deployed to restore order. Even so, some half a million refugees fled the fighting and a new wave of ethnic pogroms by both Armenians and Azeris. What was most significant, though, was the extent to which the Party leaderships on both sides were themselves jumping on the nationalist bandwagon. Both republics declared their sovereignty, and both began building up what were in effect their own armies, expanding and arming so-called 'special police forces' and similar private militias.

It was not only within the Soviet borders that an old empire was shaking. Gorbachev had come to realize that the days of Soviet military control of Eastern Europe were over. The USSR could not afford to maintain more than half a million soldiers in the region, especially not now that many of these states were themselves either on the verge of bankruptcy (and the Soviet coffers could hardly bail them out as they had in the past) or actively opposed to *perestroika* (as in East Germany and Romania). Instead, he sought to cut his losses and try to make some political capital out of withdrawal, just as he had in pulling Soviet troops out of their no-win war in Afghanistan. In December 1988, he had used the occasion of a speech to the United Nations General Assembly to announce a unilateral cut in the Soviet army of half a million troops. They were going to have to come from somewhere, and so 1989 was thus also the year of the so-called 'velvet revolutions' of Eastern Europe. As the USSR withdrew its military, political and economic support from its puppet states, some willingly embraced reform, others simply collapsed. The Berlin Wall fell in November to be followed by the East German regime. The same month a reformist government was installed in Czechoslovakia. In Romania, Ceausescu's brutal neo-Stalinist regime was toppled by a combined popular uprising and military coup, probably with Moscow's hidden support.

The 'War of the Presidents': Gorbachev's Bitter Triumph

The story of the final years of the USSR is thus also a story of the resurgence of nationalism in the regions it had once controlled. This was perhaps most strikingly true in Russia itself, and it was the rise of Russian, anti-Party nationalism which ultimately doomed Gorbachev and his hopes. In 1989, Gorbachev had been elected Chair of the Supreme Soviet and thus in effect the President of the USSR. He was not to find this the powerful positon he had hoped. Instead, he found himself presiding over a period of political and economic chaos. Reform had disorganized the planned economy, but left the institutions of the old system powerful enough to frustrate the emergence of a viable market alternative. The budget deficit rose steadily and in response all the government could do was print more money. More money chasing fewer goods just fuelled inflation. As the political system fragmented, so too did the structures of tax collection. In 1990–1, the central government only received just over a third the revenue it had expected, further limiting its ability to govern. By the end of 1989, some 90 per cent of people had taken to hoarding goods, unsure if even basic necessities would continue to be available.

In part as a result of this general crisis of governance, Gorbachev decided to create a new 'Executive Presidency', in effect granting himself far wider powers. Where the elections had failed to create the strong, stable basis for reform, instead he would take the whole burden upon himself. This represented an important change of direction, for whereas before, *demokratizatsiya* had been heading, however imperfectly, towards a parliamentary system of government, now the foundations were laid for a strongly presidential form of government. Although it is possible to see Gorbachev's logic, the result was not only to create the possible basis for a future return to authoritarianism but also to divert attention away from actually getting the parliamentary system working. The preparedness to change his ideas and adopt new strategies which could be one of Gorbachev's greatest strengths could also mean that he failed to perservere when things did not go well from the first.

In March 1990, the Congress of People's Deputies duly elected him to this new post, with 71 per cent of the vote. His trumph was short-lived, though. In May, Boris Yeltsin was also elected into a newly created office, that of the President of the Russian Federation. Although the USSR was officially a federation of equal partners, it had always been Russian-dominated. Proof of this had been the very weakness of distinctively Russian as opposed to Soviet institutions. There was no specifically Russian KGB, for example, while the Russian republican ministries had a far closer relationship with the All-Union counterparts than, say, those of the Ukraine or Turkmenistan. Capitalizing on their successes in the elections, though, the radicals had begun creating their own 'state-within-a-state'. As hitherto passive Russian political structures began to be turned into genuine organs of government, the Soviet government faced a new challenge, right at its heart. From the Russian parliament building – the so-called 'White House' – Yeltsin launched a 'war of laws', a sustained and often effective campaign to usurp central powers. Nor were the radicals alone in using Russia as a base for resistance to Gorbachev. In 1990, hard-liners established the Communist Party of the Russian Socialist Federal Soviet Republic as a bastion of conservatism within the CPSU.

The era of *demokratizatsiya* had thus radically changed the whole basis of Soviet politics and made inevitable its steady fragmentation. Perhaps most importantly, it created a new type of politics which explicitly played not to Gorbachev's strengths but his limitations. Himself a master of behind-the-scenes political manipulation, he could not adjust either to losing the political initiative or to the new realities of democratic politics. He was used to dealing with small numbers of fellow politicians, whom he could manoeuvre, win over or marginalize. He was never able to play to a mass audience, though: his speeches were long and thin on both substance and excitement, and his personal instincts out of tune with those of his people. The product of a sheltered Party lifestyle, he could not understand the desperation of the hungry and hopeless Soviet people. A Soviet nationalist, he could not come to terms with the new nationalisms which flared up across the Union, and the anger of peoples under Russian control for decades or centuries.

Reading and Sources

Gorbachev's constitutional experiment has been widely analysed: John Miller's *Mikhail Gorbachev and the End of Soviet Power*, Richard Sakwa's *Gorbachev and his Reforms, 1985–1990* and Rachel Walker's *Six Years That Shook the World* are especially acute in their judgements. Boris Yeltsin's rather blunter assessments are to be found in his autobiographical *Against the Grain*. For a conservative critique, the 'Andreyeva letter' has been reprinted in both David Lane's *Soviet Society under Perestroika* (1992, Routledge) and *The Soviet System in Crisis*, edited by Alexander Dallinn and Gail Lapidus.

As regards other issues of the time, the end of the USSR's Eastern European empire is well-discussed in Karen Dawisha's *Eastern Europe, Gorbachev and Reform*, and, from a more directly

'Muscovite' perspective, in Coit Blacker's *Hostage to Revolution* (1993, Council on Foreign Relations Press). *The Soviet Transition* (1993, Frank Cass), a collection of articles from *The Journal of Communist Studies*, edited by Stephen White, Rita di Leo and Ottorino Cappelli, also contains several useful pieces. Neil Robinson's and Ottorino Cappelli's articles on the USSR's flirtation with parliamentary democracy are good, but there are also helpful studies of economic reform, the media and ethnic conflict. The most compelling study of the way nationalism rose in the USSR remains Hélène Carrère d'Encausse's *The End of the Soviet Empire* (1993, Basic Books), although at times she writes with more vigour than accuracy.

7

GORBACHEV THE REVOLUTIONARY: THE END OF THE SOVIET UNION

In late 1990, feeling trapped and politically impotent, Gorbachev considered cutting a deal with conservatives in the Party, army and KGB. The period of this 'winter alliance' saw a marked swing back towards the use of threat and violence in a vain attempt to restore the powers of the centre. Gorbachev never really had the heart and stomach to be a dictator, though. Massive protests in Moscow in March 1991 catalysed his doubts about his new allies. He thus turned instead towards constructing a new basis for the USSR through negotiations with elected republican leaders, including Boris Yeltsin. This 'betrayal' triggered the August coup, when a collection of the leaders of the Old Guard tried to hold the Union together – and in doing so doomed it. The coup was defeated, but this was not to prove a victory for Gorbachev. Instead, it led to the end of the USSR, its fragmentation into new, often unstable states and the dissolution of the CPSU. Perhaps this was inevitable. It is hard to see how Gorbachev could have achieved his dream of a reformed, modernized and dynamic USSR still within the grip of the Party and Marxism–Leninism. In many ways, *perestroika* fits neatly into centuries-old patterns of Russian history, of cycles of attempted reform, chaos and then conservative reaction. Yet, as will be discussed at the end of this chapter, Gorbachev's painful revolution can be regarded as a distinctive phenomenon.

The 'Winter Alliance'

For some time, hard-liners within the Party had sought to persuade Gorbachev to adopt a less radical strategy. Above all, they hoped to convince him to return to a more Andropovian line, of concentrating upon economic development rather than across-the-board reform of all aspects of the Soviet system. It would be easy to dismiss them either as nostalgic dinosaurs or sly wreckers hoping to derail *perestroika*, but their arguments did have some merit. It was certainly true that democratization had not relegitimized the Soviet state or given Gorbachev a new mandate to reform. Instead, it had created a stalemate, in which the government could not govern. Something certainly needed to be done about that, just as it was right to highlight the problems of the economy. Democracy plus poverty is the recipe not so much for civilized development as for dictatorship. Furthermore, it is possible to identify states which appear to have been able to reconcile political authoritarianism with dynamic economic growth. One of the more surreal aspects of *glasnost'* in 1990 and 1991 was to see orthodox Communists praising the examples of their ideological rival China, the US ally South Korea and Chile in the time of the right-wing military dictator General Pinochet.

Beneath the surface, many of these arguments broke down, not least because the USSR was not China (where the political elite had never lost political control in the first place), nor South Korea (with its US support and still strong authoritarian tradition) nor Chile (with its united security forces and conservative elites). There was enough in such siren calls, though, that Gorbachev could be briefly tempted in the winter of 1990–1. It is still difficult to be precise about the exact order of events, not least because this was no open shift in policy, more a gradual and often grudging realignment in political loyalties. What is clear is that following the election of Boris Yeltsin as President of Russia in May 1990, Gorbachev became increasingly disillusioned with his programme of democratization. It hardly helped that the May Day parade on the Party's day of celebration witnessed crowds in Red Square jeering Gorbachev and the other leaders, waving banners reading 'Seventy-Two

Years on the Road to Nowhere' and 'Gorbachev Resign'. Television viewers saw an angry Gorbachev stare down stonily, fidget a while and then lead his colleagues off their reviewing stand. Although 'insulting the President' was promptly made a criminal offence, Gorbachev had clearly been bested by the crowd. He concentrated his energies on foreign affairs, but could not even derive the solace and support·from this that once he could. The year was dominated by the reunification of Germany, something which dismayed not just the hard-liners but many ordinary Soviet citizens with memories of the Second World War. Western aid, that mythical Holy Grail of the reformers, never materialized on anything like the scale they had hoped.

At the XXVIII Party Congress in July, Gorbachev managed to push through some important organizational reforms, but he also had to put up with several reverses and embarrassments. In June, a hard-line critic of *perestroika*, Ivan Polozkov, had been elected First Secretary of the newly founded Russian Federation Communist Party within the CPSU, suggesting a growing hostility to reform in the ranks. This was evident at the Congress when Gorbachev's mentor, Alexander Yakovlev, failed to be elected to the Central Committee. Meanwhile, the radicals within the Party continued to make life difficult for him, rather than providing him any support. Most dramatically, Yeltsin used the podium of the Congress to announce his long-awaited split with the Party. He then left the chamber, followed by an array of other radical figures, including Gavriil Popov and Anatoli Sobchak, respectively the mayors of Moscow and Leningrad. Overall, the XXVIII Congress was a bitter and rancorous affair, which did Gorbachev little good. It certainly made it clear that the discipline and unity of the Party was a thing of the past.

Gorbachev was visibly depressed, tired and short-tempered. This was the time at which the new alliance was agreed. In September, there was even a brief scare when it appeared that a military coup was in the making. Combat-ready paratroopers were airlifted unannounced to the outskirts of Moscow. Defence Minister Yazov unconvincingly claimed that they were just helping out with the potato harvest – fully armed? – and the troops were promptly withdrawn. In hindsight, this may have been a show of strength to convince Gorbachev or it may have been a trial run, the first evidence of the alliance. Either way, by October, a team within the General Staff's Main Operations Directorate was updating 'Operation Snowstorm', a long-standing emergency plan for declaring martial law. Generally, there seemed a new mood in the air. Conservative figures who previously had been full of doom and gloom suddenly seemed heartened, and reformists within the government began finding their efforts thwarted by a sudden absence of political support from the top. Having been encouraged to create a plan for a rapid transition to a market economy, Stanislav Shatalin presented his '500 Days' programme in August. Gorbachev equivocated and then ditched the plan, effectively closing the door to major economic reform. Interior Minister Vadim Bakatin, an earnest and loyal reformer who had tried to turn the police force from being a tool of the Party to a servant of the law, was sacked. In his place Gorbachev appointed Boris Pugo, a hard-line KGB officer with a tough reputation. For his deputy, Pugo was given Colonel Boris Gromov, a former commander of forces in Afghanistan. Together, the secret policeman and the general began militarizing the Interior Ministry, reversing or blocking many of the reforms Bakatin had introduced. Gennadi Yanayev, a grey caricature of the old-style conservative Party bureaucrat, was appointed Vice President. The long-serving Nikolai Ryzhkov was replaced as Prime Minister by Valentin Pavlov, the former Minister of Finance.

In December, Foreign Minister Eduard Shevardnadze resigned, warning of 'the advance of dictatorship'. The departure of a respected liberal and, more importantly, a long-time ally of Gorbachev's, underlined the extent to which the President had changed course. In the rebellious Baltic states, political attacks on local nationalist leaderships began to be supplemented by direct measures. In the capitals of Latvia and Lithuania, OMON riot police seized important buildings. Gorbachev then demanded that the Lithuanian parliament in effect renounce their claims that Soviet rule over the country was illegitimate, based, as it was, on military conquest. When they refused, OMON and KGB commandos stormed first the Lithuanian TV centre and then the headquarters of the Latvian Interior Ministry. Eighteen people died, and the coming months saw a rising tide of state authoritarianism throughout the USSR. In some cases, this was in the form of overt government measures, such as new decrees which put thousands of troops on to the streets, notionally to help fight crime. There was also a rolling campaign of scarcely hidden intimidation intended to warn the faint-hearted away from nationalist activity.

The 'winter alliance' was always a fragile and conditional one, though. Gorbachev did not trust or especially like his new allies. While prepared to entrust the Interior Ministry to them, for example, he refused to carry out a major reshuffle within the military, which would prove very important in determining the outcome of the 1991 coup attempt. Even with Shevardnadze gone, there were those within his circle warning him of the dangers and limitations in this alliance, let alone any attempt to reverse democratization. In March, they were able to make their case. First of all, when a national miners' strike paralysed the Soviet coal industry, although some hard-liners talked of sending in the riot police to break the demonstrations, it was clear that there was little they could do to convince the workers to return to the pits. In the end, it was Boris Yeltsin who managed to broker a truce. Not only did the 'winter alliance' offer no real solution to such problems as labour protests, it was downright dangerous. This was brought home by a protest march in March called in support of Boris Yeltsin, at the time facing criticism from hard-liners in the Russian parliament. The march was banned, but the organizers decided to hold it all the same. On the day, perhaps 500 000 marchers were faced by around 50 000 police and troops. In the event, it passed off relatively peacefully. The authorities settled for moving the march away from the vicinity of the Red Square and preventing any over-large concentrations forming, while the protesters were happy to have made their point. Nevertheless, while the hard-liners were triumphant, Gorbachev was sobered both by the strength of the support the radicals could muster and the danger of the situation. What would have happened, Yakovlev asked him, if something had gone wrong and a single marcher had been killed? All Moscow would have turned out for the funeral and the radicals would have had a martyr. The hard-liners had been telling Gorbachev that the marchers planned to storm the Kremlin and had even equipped themselves with siege ladders and climbing ropes. At the time he had swallowed their lies. After the protest, though, he came to realize that not only did he run a grave danger of becoming simply the puppet of his new allies, but that their plans could too easily tear the country in civil war. He moved quickly to disengage himself and resume contacts with liberals and republican nationalist leaders.

Coming off the Fence

By renouncing the 'winter alliance', Gorbachev had sealed his fate, and that of the CPSU and USSR alike. It is going too far to suggest that he had burnt all his bridges: even when they launched their coup attempt in August, hard-liners still clearly hoped that he could be induced to join them and lend his authority to their declaration of martial law. But it did represent the point at which Gorbachev finally accepted that he had to come off the fence. In 1991, he at last showed himself prepared to defy his critics within the CPSU – albeit he never lost his hopes that he could ultimately reform the institution itself – and strike a radical, even revolutionary deal with the new generation of radical and nationalist politicians which would transform the very nature of the Soviet state.

The 'winter alliance' had always, after all, been a rather awkward one. Gorbachev had never been very comfortable in bed with the military and security interests. He had not even served his national service and even if democratization were to be reversed, there was no escaping the economic logic which dictated sharp reductions in the defence budget. Perhaps most importantly, Gorbachev was poorly suited to the use of coercion. Gorbachev was heir to a tradition of rule stretching from Tsars through General Secretaries, in which force and oppression were seen as common, even natural instruments of the state. Gorbachev had his share of blood on his hands, but not only was he by inclination unhappy with the use of violence, his skills were those of the politician and publicist.

Instead, then, in April Gorbachev brought the 'winter alliance' to a conclusive end. He opened talks with the leaders of Russia, Ukraine, Kazakhstan, Belorussia, Azerbaijan, Kirghizia, Tajikistan, Turkmenistan and Uzbekistan, the so-called '9+1' talks (also called the 'Novo-Ogarevo' talks after the place they met). These talks were intended to pave the way towards a new agreement between the centre and the republics, discussed in the next section. As such, it represented a dramatic shift on Gorbachev's part towards the radicals and nationalists. They were secret, but at this time the KGB was bugging Gorbachev, and so the hard-liners soon knew what was going on. Gorbachev's relations with the leadership of the CPSU also took a sharp turn for the worse. At a plenary meeting of the Central Committee that month, he faced an unprecedented barrage of criticism. The CPSU was, after all, in a state of rapid decline, having lost so many members that by 1991 it was actually running at a loss. Blamed for the chaos in country and Party alike, Gorbachev stormed out of the meeting, threatening to resign. Loyalists united behind him and the hard-liners backed away from the confrontation. In a way, this was a victory for Gorbachev, but a very bitter one. The hard-liners had feared an open split within the Party. They also realized that thanks to his new post as President, Gorbachev could still rule even if he resigned as General Secretary. Unsure of their strength within the country, of the mood of the Party and of the implications of an open struggle against Gorbachev, they withdrew, but only to fight another day. As for Gorbachev, while in the long term he still dreamt of a popular, democratic and reformist Communist Party, in terms of the immediate politics of the moment, he had come to see it as a purely negative force. He, too, feared the consequences if his bluff was called and he gave up the General Secretaryship. His successor would almost certainly be a hard-liner, and, as he later admitted, by then he felt he could not risk control of the Party passing out of his hands.

Given that his constitutional position gave him a power base independent of the Party, it was this that Gorbachev's opponents targeted next. This attack should have alerted him to the extent to which many of his former allies were now his enemies. In June, Prime Minister Pavlov addressed the Supreme Soviet and asked them to transfer many of the powers vested in the Presidency to himself. He claimed that this was simply a matter of administrative common sense, but few of the deputies accepted this rationale. Pavlov admitted that he had not discussed this with Gorbachev and, when asked directly if he still supported the President's reform programme, stood at the podium in awkward silence for a few moments, then cracked a smile and said that he thought he had answered that. There was rather less to smile about at a secret session held that afternoon. Kryuchkov put on a performance worthy of the Cold War days, claiming that the CIA had infiltrated the very highest echelons of the government and were using *perestroika* to undermine the USSR. He held back from accusing Gorbachev and his allies of being tools of the West, but only just.

Again, the hard-liners were to fail in direct confrontation, but again Gorbachev's victory was to be at best partial. In response, the President addressed the Supreme Soviet himself, and he was at his best. Pavlov was treated with a condescending contempt and the whole affair dismissed as a sideshow. In private, Gorbachev was not so relaxed. Yet while he hauled Pavlov, Kryuchkov and the other instigators of this plot over the coals, he did not sack or even publicly rebuke them. In part, this was the product of his own over-confidence; these men all owed their positions to him and ultimately he thought they would never dare push him too far. As usual, though, Gorbachev had not realized how far his own ideas had changed and how, like Yegor Ligachev in the early years of reform, he had left behind these people who once may have shared his dream. At the same time, though, the options open to Gorbachev were also very limited. He feared the consequences of open hostilities with the hard-liners, especially in the absence of any real support base of his own. If he was to do more than just parry the attacks of his opponents, he needed allies.

A New Beginning: the Union Treaty

To this end, Gorbachev turned to the leaders of the newly empowered republican governments. Directly elected, characteristically former Party officials who had realized the way the wind was blowing and adopted nationalist positions, they had the legitimacy Gorbachev lacked and were generally also able and willing to deal with him, if he was willing to make significant concessions. By now he was prepared to see an unprecedented degree of power pass away from the central government to the republics. While some republican leaderships were hell-bent on outright secession from the USSR, even a fractious and begrudging Boris Yeltsin was induced to join the negotiations.

At the XXVIII Party Congress in 1990, Gorbachev had admitted that inter-ethnic relations had worsened. He trailed the notion of a new Union Treaty to replace the 1922 treaty on which the USSR had originally been founded, to establish a 'real union of sovereign states'. Although work had been done later that year to begin to turn this hazy idea into reality, largely by demarking the powers of the centre and the republics more clearly, there was clearly little political momentum behind the idea. A rather unsatisfactory draft Union Treaty was published in November, but all but forgotten given that a central theme of the 'winter alliance' was the need to recentralize power in the USSR, not devolve it. At the time, Gorbachev was clearly disassociating himself from the idea. In October he had warned against a 'Lebanonization' of the country which would see it torn by civil wars. In December, he went on to announce a USSR-wide referendum on the future of the Soviet state. This was held on 17 March 1991, but the question posed was hopelessly biased: 'Do you consider it necessary to preserve the USSR as a renewed federation of equal sovereign republics in which the human rights and freedoms of any nationality will be fully guaranteed?' Faced with the option of voting 'yes' to the status quo, or 'no' and perhaps appear to be attacking equal rights and freedom, not surprisingly many dissenters did not bother voting. Six republican governments – the Baltic states, Moldavia, Georgia and Armenia – refused to hold the referendum altogether, and so overall turnout was around 80 per

113

cent. As a result, the 'yes' vote was 76.4 per cent, yet this was hardly a mandate for anything useful.

Nevertheless, this draft Union Treaty did provide the initial basis on which to begin negotiations with the republican leaders. The negotiations were difficult, but by the end of July there was at least a working text on which Gorbachev, Yeltsin and four other republican leaders could agree. The new treaty would create a 'Union of Soviet Sovereign (as opposed to Socialist) Republics', and envisaged the devolution of a truly impressive range of powers to the republics. The four key elements of the new treaty were:

• Voluntary membership. Republics would be free to join or decide to go their own way. Gorbachev was thus accepting the claims for complete independence made by Georgia, Latvia, Lithuania and Estonia and, to a lesser extent, Moldavia and Armenia.
• Republican sovereignty. In a reversal of existing practice, republican law would take precedence over All-Union law.
• Devolved taxation. The central government would not have an independent tax base and instead depend upon funding from the republics. Given that money is the fuel for any government, it meant that the republics would have the right to determine the central government's competencies and capabilities.
• Limited central bodies. There would be no All-Union parliament, with the USSR Supreme Soviet being disbanded, and while there would still be central armed forces and security services, these would be much smaller than their Soviet counterparts and subject to oversight by republican legislatures. All-Union ministries would generally either be dissolved or turned into much smaller co-ordinating bodies, largely supporting republican ministries.

To many within the Party and state leadership, this new treaty was a recipe for disaster. First of all, it would destroy the old USSR without any concrete vision of what would replace it. The treaty did not, for example, expressly describe what powers would remain at the centre, and failed to cover a variety of knotty questions, such as how to resolve inter-republican disputes. Furthermore, only five republics were definitely prepared to sign: Russia, Kazakhstan, Uzbekistan, Tajikistan and Belorussia. Although this represented a sizeable bloc (and the majority of the land area of the USSR), especially given that, for all its indecision, Ukraine would probably also join, it nevertheless meant an end to an empire centuries in the making. To conservatives, this was also a betrayal of the March referendum.

It also had serious implications for the very interest groups to be represented by the men who organized the coup in August. The KGB would be purged and cut down dramatically in size and powers. While individual republics retained their own security services, the central KGB – like the central Interior Ministry – would become little more than a glorified secretariat involved in the sharing of information. As for KGB Chair Kryuchkov himself, Yeltsin and Kazakh President Nursultan Nazarbayev had made it clear to Gorbachev that he would have to go. A central army would survive, but this would be a far smaller and less ambitious organization, essentially a defensive force. The powerful and pampered defence industries could certainly no longer expect the huge orders and subsidies to which they were still accustomed. Indeed, the whole central economic planning and support system would not survive. As the republics moved towards a market economy, inefficient, loss-making farms and factories would finally be forced to close. The huge army of Party economic bureaucrats (from whom Prime Minister Pavlov had been drawn) would find their careers coming to an abrupt halt. The Communist Party of the Soviet Union itself could hardly survive without fragmenting into smaller, republican parties and, without its guaranteed grip on the state, facing the challenge of more popular political rivals.

The August Coup

The new Union Treaty, Gorbachev's last hope of reforming and saving the USSR, thus ultimately proved its undoing. By managing to thwart the hard-liners' constitutional attempts to block reform, he left them no option but unconstitutional

115

measures. By promoting them when they were useful but not removing them when they became a threat, Gorbachev allowed them to launch their abortive coup from within the state and even gave them some hope he would throw his weight behind them if they succeeded. By failing either to convince them of the necessity of the concessions he wrote into the Union Treaty and giving so many within the Party, economic and security lobbies no hope for their post-treaty careers, Gorbachev gave them no real alternative but to try and block it.

Again in hindsight, the surprise is not that the hard-liners launched a coup so much as that anyone should be surprised that they did. Not only were their interests clearly at stake, but there had been ample forewarning. In July, the conservative newspaper *Sovetskaya Rossiya* carried an open letter from 12 leading figures, including two of the eventual leaders of the coup, Alexander Tizyakov and Vasili Starodubtsev. Headed 'A Word to the People', it called for the establishment of a state of emergency in the country and, in effect, the removal of Yeltsin and his allies. On 13 August, Pavlov would warn that the Union Treaty would create administrative and economic anarchy. As late as 15 August, Yakovlev would be predicting that a 'Stalinist grouping' was readying a 'party and state coup'.

Even so, with Russia, Kazakhstan and Uzbekistan due to be the first to sign the new Union Treaty on the 20th of the month, on 4 August, Gorbachev left for a brief holiday in the Crimea. On 16 August, the final draft of the Union Treaty was published, and the following day, four of the leading lights of the coup – Pavlov, Kryuchkov, Yazov and Yanayev – met at a secret KGB safe house to discuss its implications. They were joined by Anatoli Lukyanov, the Chairman of the USSR Supreme Soviet. A long-time friend of his, Lukyanov was another prime example of an ally left behind as Gorbachev became increasingly radical. With Lukyanov refusing to support them directly but lending his moral support, the four agreed that the treaty had to be stopped.

It is clear that this was a difficult decision and that, for all their rattling of sabres, they had never expected to have to take it. If nothing else, this is shown by the hurried and haphazard nature of their organization, having to throw a plan together and carry it out in a bare couple of days. They still hoped to have Gorbachev's sanction, a sign of the extent to which he shaped and dominated a whole generation of Soviet leaders. Indeed, most saw his preparedness to compromise and make concessions not as the mark of a wily politician but as a sign of essential weakness, a willingness to capitulate to whoever seemed the strongest. By presenting him with an ultimatum, they felt they could bring him on board. On 18 August, they sent a delegation to Gorbachev's holiday villa at Foros. It included Valeri Boldin, Gorbachev's chief of staff, army commander General Valentin Varennikov, Oleg Baklanov, First Vice Chair of the Defence Council and General Yuri Plekhanov, Gorbachev's chief of security. They asked Gorbachev to sanction martial law. Baklanov suggested 'you take a rest and while you're away, we'll do the dirty work.' Failing that, they demanded he resign. His reply was robust: 'You will destroy yourselves, but that's your business and to hell with you. But you will also destroy the country and everything we have already done.' The delegation withdrew, and Gorbachev and his family and retinue found themselves prisoners in the villa, their radio and telephone links broken.

On Monday 19 August, the Soviet people woke to the news that the President was 'ill' and that a State Committee for the State of Emergency (GKChP) was running the country in his absence. This committee comprised eight people: the original four plotters, Yanayev, Pavlov, Yazov and Kryuchkov, plus Baklanov, Pugo and two representatives of the economic bureaucracy: Tizyakov, president of the Association of State Enterprises, and Starodubtsev, chair of the Party-controlled Peasants' Union. The committee declared a state of emergency and issued an appeal for national support strikingly similar to the rhetoric of 'A Word to the People'. It certainly did not say much about the Party or socialism. Instead, it was couched in very nationalist terms, promising a restoration of order, discipline and national pride to the USSR. This was actually a very negative and even defeatist effort. The plotters feared the new Union Treaty and all it would mean for them. They resented what they saw as the squandering of the USSR's military and political resources in pursuit of Western aid and recognition.

They were appalled by the rise of all sorts of new social phenomena, from crime and anti-Soviet nationalism to grass-roots political activism and entrepreneurship. Yet they had no real answers, no credible alternatives. In many ways they had made three reckless gambles:

- that Gorbachev would accept their initiative and provide the leadership for their emergency regime;
- that they would maintain the loyalty of the security forces; and
- perhaps most importantly, that they would face no real opposition.

As Yazov later admitted, they had simply anticipated that the Soviet people would accept their decrees. All three gambles proved seriously misjudged. Without Gorbachev, the GKChP's claim to legitimate authority over the security forces was dubious. There were units and commanders whose loyalties were with the nationalists and radicals, some of whom proved to have a vital role. Air force commander Colonel General Yevgeni Shaposhnikov, for example, refused to support the coup, while paratroop commander Colonel General Pavel Grachev contrived to keep his troops out of Moscow and even sent a small contingent to guard the 'White House', Boris Yeltsin's parliament building. There were also loyal Soviet commanders who had little sympathy for the radicals but refused to accept their plotters' authority. One such was Major General Alexander Lebed', whose refusal to storm the 'White House' effectively doomed the plotters' hopes of a military solution to Yeltsin's resistance. With the officer corps divided, the army was effectively paralysed, waiting to see if the GKChP could carry off its adventure. Nor were the police or KGB any more useful to the plotters. Although Kryuchkov was a key member of the GKChP, most parts of the KGB were torn by internal divisions or had even decided to throw in their lot with the nationalists, convinced the coup would fail. Overall, though, there probably would have been sufficient elements within the army and security forces prepared to enforce the GKChP's writ had there been the will to use them ruthlessly. The Dzerzhinsky Division, a special security force based in Moscow, was prepared for action, while the *Al'fa* commando unit which eventually refused a suicide mission to storm the 'White House' had been in place and ready to arrest Yeltsin on the first morning of the coup had the orders been given. Instead, the muddled uncertainty of the security forces largely reflected the mood at the top. The civilian members of the GKChP spent most of their time drunk or bickering and showed little inclination to trigger a civil war. Yazov, in particular, was a half-hearted conspirator from the first and held back from agreeing to use force to impose martial law.

The fact is that coups generally succeed thanks to momentum. Even the handful of forces at the GKChP's disposal might have been enough had they been used forcefully and had they faced minimal opposition. With most people in the country adopting a 'wait and see' approach in the first few days of the coup, though, the plotters' muddled uncertainty stood in stark contrast to the vigour and unity of the resistance they faced. Having evaded arrest on that fateful first morning, Boris Yeltsin made it to the 'White House', which he made a focus of public resistance to the coup. He roundly denounced it as illegal and called an emergency meeting of the Russian parliament. Reformists ranging from Shevardnadze and Yakovlev to the Patriarch of the Russian Orthodox Church and Yelena Bonner, wife of Andrei Sakharov, united behind Yeltsin. After a shaky start, as it became clear that the GKChP could not or would not crush this resistance, more and more leaders and groups came off the fence and declared their opposition to the coup, even including the CPSU. In many of the republics, this provided a catalyst for independence, as national presidents took over functions previously controlled by the centre. The momentum was clearly with the opposition.

Torn by indecision, unprepared for a bloodbath and lacking any coherent programme, the GKChP soon disintegrated. Shortly after noon on 21 August, the plotters left Moscow to fly to Foros, apparently hoping to throw themselves on Gorbachev's mercy. On their tail was a jet containing Russian Vice President Alexander Rutskoi and a security team. Gorbachev refused to see the plotters and was brought back to Moscow by Rutskoi, arriving the next day. The plotters were arrested, with the exception of Pugo, who committed suicide.

An Appraisal: the Reluctant Revolutionary

Yet Gorbachev returned to a very different country, and the coup proved crucial in finally tilting the balance of power away from him and his hopes of a renewed Union and towards the republican leaders, and Boris Yeltsin in particular. Ruthless in victory, Yeltsin suspended the activities of the Party inside Russia and publicly forced Gorbachev to accept the legality of a series of decrees the Russian government made during the coup, including the transfer of economic enterprises and resources on Russian soil to its jurisdiction. Although on 24 August, Gorbachev resigned as General Secretary of the CPSU, it was too late for him to disassociate himself from the Party he had for years tried to reform and which had become identified with the GKChP. The whole USSR was unravelling before his eyes, and he was powerless to stop it. The Ukraine declared independence, followed by most of the remaining republics. While Gorbachev tried desperately to breathe life back into his 'Union of Soviet Sovereign Republics', with Yeltsin so clearly set on full independence for Russia, it had little chance. When Yeltsin further proposed an even looser 'Commonwealth of Independent States', a general alliance between countries with no central government (and thus, no role for Gorbachev), he had to accept he was beaten. On 25 December, he signed his final decree, divesting himself of the office of Soviet President, and on 31 December 1991, the USSR was formally dissolved.

This book has tried to present an analytical narrative of the last decade of the Soviet Union through the medium of one person, and thus it is fair to try to set Mikhail Gorbachev's role and history in context. It would be easy to characterize him as a glorious failure. After all, in 1985 he set out to modernize and strengthen the Communist Party and the Soviet Union, and within six and a half years had destroyed them both. Institutions which had survived for 70 years, Stalin's fratricidal purges and the Nazi war machine notwithstanding, proved unable to survive well-meant reform. Yet to understand what Gorbachev did accomplish, one has to appreciate both how his ideas changed and what the longer-term implications of his revolution were. After all, Gorbachev took power at a pivotal moment in Soviet history. As an unscientific but perhaps interesting exercise in historical speculation, one can identify other possible routes which could have been taken:

- The 'Andropov' variant. Had Andropov survived, he might have presided over a more ruthless and rational economic modernization, in which attempts either to hinder reform by passive resistance or broaden it out into a political process would have had short shrift. The experience of China shows that while in the longer term, economic development appears to corrode a one-party state and its central control, meanwhile it is possible to modernize such a system from within. Who knows: such a purged and relaunched USSR might well have survived into the twenty-first century?

- The 'Romanov' variant. Of course, discipline could have been taken too far. A General Secretary such as Romanov, keen to crack the whip yet without a notion of when to compromise, might have pushed the USSR into civil war. Instead of what was – by the standards of imperial collapses – the remarkably bloodless transition of 1991, the world might have been faced with a continent-sized war-zone, bristling with rival leaders, ethnic hatred and, worst of all, uncontrolled nuclear weapons.

- The 'Grishin' variant. 'Business as usual' might have kept the USSR going a while longer. It is hard to believe that the Brezhnevite order would not have ground to a halt had Grishin or some other conservative not taken over the General Secretaryship. Nevertheless, this might well have been a slow process. Had the leadership managed to be sensible enough to have reduced certain needless commitments (such as in Afghanistan and the maintenance of client states across the globe) and to accept that the arms race was not worth winning, then, who knows, the Soviet Union could conceivably have lasted in the absence of a serious challenge either at home or abroad.

To some, Gorbachev remains an essentially transitional figure given that he regarded political reform purely as a means to modernizing the economy and not an end in itself. This is perhaps a little unfair, because while he certainly wanted to reform the USSR's economic base, Gorbachev was an evolutionary politician. In other words, while remaining true to a general ideal, he was able to develop and grow politically as he faced new challenges and was forced to accept new realities. In 1985, for example, his wife Raisa appears to have been the more radical of the two. By 1991, in contrast, she had been left behind, unable – like so many of Gorbachev's one-time colleagues and allies – to adapt with him. Having started out as a creative but essentially conformist Soviet patriot and Party loyalist, he became increasingly aware of just how far neither the USSR nor the CPSU were suitable vessels for the humanist values he still held. By the end of 1991, he appears to have been prepared to put those values above the institutions which had shaped his life. This ability to grow politically – even if Gorbachev never managed to come to terms either with economics or the human aspirations of his people – is far from common amongst leaders. As of writing at the beginning of 1996, for example, it has become clear that if anyone is a transitional figure, it is his rival and successor Boris Yeltsin, who while well able to destroy the old order, has been unable to create a new one.

In November 1990, though, Gorbachev affirmed that 'the most important revolution' was the 'revolution in minds, in our heads, in us ourselves'. In this respect, the legacy of his revolution should perhaps be seen in terms of the longer-term implications of his revolution, some of which he sought and others he never expected. These include:

- An opportunity to redefine the relationship between state and society. A state with centuries-long traditions of authoritarianism has been exposed more deeply and more extensively than ever before to the ideas and ideals of democracy and social and political pluralism. Institutions from the press to the judiciary have had the opportunity to develop a role not as agents of the elite but as independent guardians of social autonomy.
- An opportunity to redefine Russia's relationship with Europe. The USSR was heir to many of tsarist Russia's suspicions of Europe, not without reason given the intervention of

foreign troops to fight the Bolsheviks in the 1918–21 Civil War and the Nazi invasion of 1941–4. Today's Russians, though, have the opportunity to see the West not merely as a model of a desirable commercial lifestyle and pluralist politics but as an ally in creating a new Russian identity.

- The end of the Russian empire. The USSR also inherited the tsarist empire. This has crumbled, and instead of one empire there are new 15 new states, each with its own distinct identity and future.

In fairness, though, it is finally worth questioning the precise nature and extent of the changes which have taken place. One of the tragedies or ironies of the entire Soviet era is that despite the high ideals of the revolutionaries who took over in 1917, over the years their new order came increasingly to resemble the old tsarist one. Traditional ways of running the country, traditional attitudes towards the non-Russian population, even traditional security ambitions in Europe and Asia all re-emerged. So, too, are there closer parallels between the new Russia and the Soviet state from which it emerged than many would like to accept. There is a new class of business entrepreneurs and political leaders, but many are simply *apparatchiki* who have adjusted to the new rules of the game. Former Prime Minister Pavlov, for example, is now a well-paid economic consultant, while the government is full of former Soviet officials. After a brief flurry of apparent reform, the KGB has reasserted itself under new names and new guises, while the Russian army is as over-sized and over-expensive as its Soviet counterpart. The empire may be gone, but Moscow still uses its political, military and economic clout to dominate its new neighbours. The above list is simply of historical *opportunities* Gorbachev's revolution offered Russia. It may be that Russia is still not ready, able or willing to take them.

Reading and Sources

Much has been written about the events leading up to the 1991 coup. Although I may not agree with all her assessments, Rachel Walker's *Six Years That Shook the World* does present a useful summary (for a more detailed exposition of my own line, see my *The Age of Anxiety*). Caroline Schofield's *The Russian Elite* includes a fascinating soldiers'-eye account of those confused days, while *Russia at the Barricades*, edited by Victoria Bonnell, Ann Cooper and Gregory Freidin, brings together many contemporary accounts, from the press and from participants on both sides of those barricades. Mikhail Gorbachev's *The August Coup* is based on notes he wrote at the time, and while hardly a work of great literature, it does shed some light on his desperate efforts to keep alive a project already all but dead. Two postscript episodes to the BBC's excellent documentary season, *The Second Russian Revolution*, remain the best TV sources (Yakovlev's warning to Gorbachev following the March protests cited in this chapter, for example, come from one of these programmes). A final primary source on those few, last months between the coup and the formal dissolution of the USSR is *Final Days*, elegantly written by Andrei Grachev, Gorbachev's press secretary.

And what about Gorbachev's legacy? Archie Brown's *The Gorbachev Factor* is a *tour d'horizon* from the acknowledged Grand Old Man of British Sovietology. Karen Dawisha and Bruce Parrott have prepared an excellent (and commendably quick) study of the post-Soviet order in their *Russia and the New States of Eurasia* (1994, Cambridge University Press), while Richard Sakwa has written the huge, if sometimes rather heavy-going *Russian Politics and Society* (1993, Routledge). Even so, on the whole, assessments of the new Russia are still largely in the hands of journalists (though, hack to the last, I have produced *The Kremlin's Agenda* (1995, Jane's), which summarizes my rather jaundiced views). Bruce Clark's *An Empire's New Clothes* (1995, Vantage) and John Kampfner's *Inside Yeltsin's Russia* (1994, Cassell) are the best of the batch to date.

APPENDICES

I CHRONOLOGY

Gorbachev's Early Career

2 March 1931	Born in Privolnoye, in Stavropol
1945	Joins Young Communist League
1949	Awarded Order of Red Banner of Labour
1950–5	Law student at Moscow StateUniversity
1952	Joins Communist Party
1953	Marries Raisa Maximovna Titorenko
1956	Appointed Young Communist League First Secretary for the town of Stavropol
1960	Appointed Young Communist League First Secretary for region of Stavropol
1966	Appointed Party First Secretary for town of Stavropol
	Visits France as part of a delegation
1967	Visits Italy as private tourist
1970	Appointed Party First Secretary for region of Stavropol
1976	Death of his father, Sergei
1978	Appointed Central Committee Secretary for Agriculture in Moscow
1979	Becomes candidate (non-voting) member of Politburo
1980	Becomes full (voting) member of Politburo

1982
10 November	Death of Brezhnev
12 November	Andropov becomes General Secretary

1984
9 February	Death of Andropov
13 February	Chernenko becomes General Secretary
December	Gorbachev visits UK

1985
10 March	Death of Chernenko
11 March	Gorbachev becomes General Secretary
1 July	Gromyko becomes Chair of the Presidium of the Supreme Soviet (President); Shevardnadze replaces him as Foreign Minister
27 September	Ryzhkov replaces Tikhonov as Chair of the Council of Ministers (Prime Minister)
18–21 November	Geneva summit with Reagan
24 December	Yeltsin appointed Moscow Party First Secretary

1986
25 February–6 March	XXVII Party Congress
26 April	Chernobyl' disaster
11–12 October	Reykjavik summit with Reagan
19 December	Andrei Sakharov freed from internal exile

1987
27–28 January	Central Committee plenum
26 May	Law on Co-Operatives passed
28 May	Matthias Rust lands light plane in Red Square: pretext for the replacement of Sokolov with Yazov as Defence Minister
25–26 June	Central Committee plenum: adopts economic reform programme

1 July	Law on State Enterprises passed
11 November	Yeltsin replaced by Zaikov as Moscow Party First Secretary
8–10 December	Washington summit with Reagan: INF arms treaty signed

1988

20 February	Nagorno-Karabakh votes to secede from Azerbaijan and join Armenia, triggering a massacre of Armenians in the Azeri town of Sumgait
13 March	Andreyeva's conservative letter 'I Cannot Betray my Principles' published in *Sovetskaya Rossiya*
5 April	*Pravda* publishes counter-blast to Andreyeva
28 June–1 July	XIX Party Conference: reforms get go-ahead
29 September	Central Committee plenum: reorganization of the Secretariat includes demotion of Ligachev
1 October	Gromyko resigns, Gorbachev also takes on Presidency
1 December	Supreme Soviet passes constitutional amendments which will create a new parliament, the Congress of People's Deputies
7 December	Gorbachev addresses the United Nations: announces unilateral troop cuts of 500 000
8 December	Earthquake in Armenia

1989

15 February	Soviet troops complete withdrawal from Afghanistan
26 March	Multi-candidate elections to the Congress of People's Deputies begin
9 April	'Tbilisi massacre' as troops kill protesters
14 April	Agreement signed on withdrawal from Afghanistan

25 April	Central Committee plenum: Gorbachev uses poor performance of conservatives in elections to sack several
25 May–9 June	First session of the Congress of People's Deputies
25 May	Gorbachev elected President of the Supreme Soviet
2–3 December	Malta summit with Bush
12–24 December	Second session of the Congress of People's Deputies
14 December	Death of Sakharov
19 December	Lithuanian Communist Party declares independence from Communist Party of the Soviet Union

1990

19 January	Troops deployed to restore order in Baku
4 February	Large pro-democracy demonstrations in Moscow
5–7 February	Central Committee plenum
4 March	Local elections in Russia
11 March	Lithuania declares full independence
12–20 March	Third Congress of People's Deputies: constitution amended to drop Article Six, guaranteeing the 'leading role' of the CPSU, and a new, executive presidency established
15 March	Gorbachev elected to the post of Executive President
29 May	Yeltsin elected President of Russia by the Russian parliament
1–3 June	Washington summit with Bush
20 June	Russian Communist Party established
2–13 July	XXVIII Party Congress: Yeltsin and other radicals leave Party
24 September	Gorbachev acquires emergency powers
7 November	May Day parade sees anti-Gorbachev demonstrators in Red Square
December	Attacks by OMON riot police in the Baltic states
20 December	Shevardnadze resigns; Ryzhkov retires

They are replaced by Alexander
Bessmertnykh and Valentin Pavlov,
respectively

27 December   Gennadi Yanayev becomes Vice President

1991

17 March   Refendendum shows 76.4 per cent in
                  favour of the continuation of the USSR
28 March   Pro-Yeltsin protest in Moscow
9 April   Georgia declares independence
23 April   '9+1' talks between Gorbachev and
                  republican presidents begin
24–25 April   Central Committee plenum: Gorbachev
                  threatens to resign when faces a barrage
                  of criticism
13 June   Yeltsin wins first direct elections to the
                  Russian presidency
17 June   Prime Minister Pavlov attempts to
                  convince parliament to transfer presi-
                  dential powers to him
18 June   Gorbachev announces success of
                  '9+1' talks
23 July   *Sovetskaya Rossiya* publishes conservative
                  open letter 'A Word to the People'
4 August   Gorbachev leaves for Crimea
19–21 August   'August coup'
24 August   Gorbachev resigns as General Secretary
6 November   Yeltsin bans Communist Party in Russia
7–8 December   Commonwealth of Independent States
                  established
25 December   Gorbachev resigns from presidency
31 December   USSR formally dissolved

II GALLERY OF MAIN CHARACTERS

Akhromeyev, Sergei   An outstanding army officer, he became Chief of the General Staff in 1984, a post he held until his resignation in 1988 in protest at proposed defence cuts. Nevertheless, he remained Gorbachev's military adviser until his suicide in 1991.

Aliyev, Geidar   Azerbaijan's first secretary 1969–82, he was a political chameleon, who courted first Brezhnev, then Andropov, rising to the Politburo in 1982.

Andropov, Yuri   Gorbachev's main patron. He headed the KGB between 1967 and 1982, during which time he modernized it and established it as a sophisticated tool of the state. He succeeded Brezhnev as General Secretary in November 1982, even though already very ill. Gorbachev soon became in effect his deputy. He died in February 1984, and although briefly succeeded by Chernenko, had managed to establish a power base for Gorbachev's own bid for the leadership.

Bakatin, Vadim   Reformist ally of Gorbachev's; Interior Minister 1989–90; briefly Chair of the KGB in 1991.

Baklanov, Oleg   One of the August coup plotters; identified with the defence industries.

Bogomolov, Oleg   Head of the Institute of the Economics of the World Socialist System.

Brezhnev, Leonid   Easy-going General Secretary of the Party between 1964 and his death in November 1982. His time in office was marked by the consumerization of Soviet life and the corruption of the elite, and is generally (if perhaps unfairly) referred to as 'the period of stagnation'.

Chebrikov, Viktor   Chair of the KGB, 1983–8. A protégé of Andropov's, he was left behind as Gorbachev became more radical. His appointment as head of a new Legal Commission in 1988 seemed to be a promotion but proved an honourable half-way house on the road to retirement.

Chernenko, Konstantin   Short-lived General Secretary who succeeding Andropov in February 1984, yet died in March 1985. Even while in power, he was too ill and too beholden to people Andropov had appointed within the government to achieve anything of note.

Gorbachev, Mikhail   Born in Stavropol, southern Russia, in 1931, Gorbachev joined the Young Communist League at an early age and went on to read law at Moscow State University, where he met his wife, Raisa. After a career as a local Party boss, he became Central Committee Secretary for Agriculture in 1978. He became right-hand man to Yurii Andropov while he was General Secretary, managed to cling on to his position during the Chernenko interregnum, and then became General Secretary himself in 1985. This post he held until 1991, until the effective dissolution of the Communist Party. He also became the first and last elected President of the USSR.

Gorbacheva, Raisa Wife of Mikhail Gorbachev. An educated and opinionated woman, with a doctorate in philosophy, she found Russian attitudes towards women counting against her when she tried to make something of her role as 'First Lady', acquiring a popular reputation as an imperious shrew. Although she lagged behind her husband's convinced conversion to reformism, he valued her opinions at every stage, and often she was his sole confidante.

Grishin, Viktor Conservative Party secretary of Moscow 1967–85 and a rival to Gorbachev in 1985.

Gromov, Boris The charismatic last commander of Soviet forces in Afghanistan, Gromov came to represent a whole generation of *afganets* officers, ensuring his political survival, despite his association with the 1991 August coup, during which time he was First Deputy Soviet Interior Minister. He went on to become Deputy Russian Defence Minister in 1992.

Gromyko, Andrei The veteran Soviet Foreign Minister until 1985 when he was made Soviet President (at that time a largely ceremonial position, without real power) and replaced by Eduard Shevardnadze. He retired in 1988 and died soon thereafter.

Kryuchkov, Vladimir One of the 1991 August coup junta. Formerly head of the KGB's First Chief Directorate (responsible for foreign espionage), he was Chair of the KGB 1988–91

Kulakov, Felix One of Gorbachev's patrons and his predecessor as First Secretary of Stavropol and later Central Committee Secretary for Agriculture until his death in 1978.

Kunayev, Dinmukhamed Party First Secretary of Kazakhstan until his ousting in 1986.

Ligachev, Yegor One of the most interesting and contradictory figures in Gorbachev's team, was a workaholic puritan with a strong and dogmatic Marxist–Leninist conviction. As Party First Secretary of Siberia in the 1970s, his protection had allowed the University of Novosibirsk to become a haven for realistic analyses of the USSR's problems. Andropov brought him to Moscow in 1983 as Central Committee Secretary for the Organization of Party Work – in effect, chief manager of Party personnel. He supported Gorbachev's election and became his second-in-command, with special responsibility for ideology, but his more disciplinarian and inflexible stand meant that Gorbachev's increasing reformism left him behind. He also broke with Boris Yeltsin, denouncing him publicly in 1988, and then became a stern critic of what he saw as Gorbachev's increasing departure from Marxist–Leninist principles.

Lukyanov, Anatoli Once-close friend and ally of Gorbachev's, but another increasingly distanced by Gorbachev's radicalization. As Chair of the Supreme Soviet 1990–1, he was to give tacit support to the August coup.

Moiseyev, Mikhail Hawkish Chief of the General Staff, 1989–91.

Nazarbayev, Nursultan Kazakh Party First Secretary 1989–91, then President of an independent Kazakhstan.

Pavlov, Valentin 1991 August coup plotter; Prime Minister 1990–91.

Plekhanov, Yuri Head of the KGB's Ninth (Bodyguards) Directorate and as such Gorbachev's chief of security until the 1991 August coup, when he sided with the plotters and led them into Gorbachev's summer house.

Polozkov, Ivan Hard-liner who headed the Russian Communist Party 1990–1.

Pugo, Boris 1991 August coup plotter; former head of the Latvian KGB; Interior Minister 1990–1; committed suicide, 1991.

Romanov, Grigori Leningrad Party First Secretary until 1983 and a rival of Gorbachev's for the General Secretaryship. Although he was associated with Andropov, this was more because of his vocal support for more discipline rather than any reformist ideas. When he stood against Gorbachev, the KGB spread rumours about his arrogance and misuse of his position, which helped secure his downfall.

Ryzhkov, Nikolai A sober and hard-working Party bureaucrat with a background in the defence industries, Ryzhkov was another of the team to whom Andropov bequeathed his hope for reform. Loyal to Gorbachev, he was his Prime Minister between 1985 and 1990, but proved to lack the imagination to push reform to its logical conclusions and thus became increasingly out of his depth.

Sakharov, Andrei Nobel laureate nuclear physicist who became a dissident, facing persecution and internal exile in the city of Gorky for his pains. Gorbachev released him in 1986 and he became the grand old man of the liberal democrats until his death in 1989.

Shevardnadze, Eduard One of the most genuinely reform-minded of all Gorbachev's allies, more liberal even than his patron. First Georgian Interior Minister (where he made a name for himself fighting corruption) and then republican Party leader 1972–85. In 1985, he became Soviet Foreign Minister 1985–90 and later President of an independent Georgia, 1992–.

Sokolov, Sergei Soviet Defence Minister 1984–7

Starodubtsev, Vasili President of the Peasants' Union and a 1991 August coup plotter.

Suslov, Mikhail Central Committee Secretary for Ideology during the late-Brezhnev era. A chilly and fiercely conservative figure, he nonetheless approved of Gorbachev's energy and honesty and supported his rise. He died in 1982, opening the way for the succession of his main rival, Andropov.

Talyzin, Nikolai Head of *Gosplan*, 1985–8, forced to resign on account of his passive sabotage of reforms.

Tikhonov, Nikolai Soviet Prime Minister until 1985.

Tizyakov, Alexander President of the Association of State Enterprises (and thus mouthpiece of the country's industrial managers); 1991 August coup plotter.

Ustinov, Dmitri Soviet Defence Minister 1976–84. He supported Andropov's election, then had his doubts about Gorbachev, backing Chernenko instead.

Varennikov, Valentin Commander-in-Chief of Ground Forces 1989–91; arrested for his role in the 1991 August coup.

Vorotnikov, Vitali Industrial administrator and Party organizer, appointed Premier of the Russian Federation under Andropov. He proved a lukewarm reformer and was replaced under Gorbachev.

Yakovlev, Alexander In many ways the spiritual father of *perestroika*, this tough-minded, obstinate but indubitably brilliant specialist in ideology and US foreign policy became Gorbachev's main adviser in 1985 and Central Committee Secretary for Ideology. He encouraged Gorbachev's democratization and his allies with the radicals in 1991.

Yanayev, Gennadi Notional leader of the 1991 August coup; a bureaucrat, who became Soviet Vice President, 1990–1 as part of Gorbachev's 'winter alliance' with conservatives.

Yazov, Dmitri Member of the 1991 August coup junta; Soviet Defence Minister 1987–91

Yeltsin, Boris Gorbachev's radical nemesis, an ex-bureaucrat who proved a very able politician and the chief beneficiary of democratization. Party First Secretary in the cities of Sverdlovsk (1976–85) and then Moscow (1986–7), he was sacked by Gorbachev when he became politically embarrassing. From this point, Yeltsin became the figurehead of liberal Russian nationalism and opposition to the Party. Elected President of the Russian Federation in 1990, he went on the lead the resistance to the 1991 August coup and ultimately dismantled both Gorbachev's Party and his Soviet Union.

Zaikov, Lev Party Secretary of Leningrad, 1983–5, then of Moscow after Yeltsin's dismissal.

BIBLIOGRAPHY AND GUIDE TO FURTHER READING

Much that is excellent (and a fair amount that is not) has been written about Gorbachev and his times. This cannot be anything other than a very selective guide to some of the best and most useful books and articles.

General texts

Brown, Archie, *The Gorbachev Factor* (1996, Oxford University Press). The latest study, from the Sovietologist who first spotted Gorbachev as the coming man to watch.

Hosking, Geoffrey, *The Awakening of the Soviet Union* (1991, Mandarin). An engaging personal overview of the era, especially looking at the evolution of Soviet society at this time.

Miller, John, *Mikhail Gorbachev and the End of Soviet Power* (1993, Macmillan).
An extremely good study, which manages both to remain sympathetic to Gorbachev and his efforts without in any way sentimentalizing him and to address complex issues without becoming confusing or over-simplified.

Sakwa, Richard, *Gorbachev and his Reforms, 1985–1990* (1990, Philip Allen).
Not the most readable book, but an intelligent and very compre-hensive survey.

Walker, Rachel, *Six Years That Shook the World* (1993, Manchester University Press).
A novel approach, which uses note-form and clear listings and sections to develop a good, wide-ranging analysis of the period.

White, Stephen, Pravda, Alex and Gitelman, Zvi (eds.), *Developments in Soviet and Post-Soviet Politics* (1992, Macmillan).
A very useful collection of articles.

Biographies and Autobiographies

Gorbachev, Mikhail, *Perestroika* (1987, Collins).

Gorbachev, Mikhail, *The August Coup* (1991, HarperCollins).
A short work knocked out very soon after the coup, it combines rather bland general statements of his views with some personal recollections. Hardly insightful, but a useful guide to his views in late 1991.

Grachev, Andrei, *Final Days* (1996, Westview).
The inside story of Gorbachev's press officer; an interesting book.

Ligachev, Yegor, *Inside Gorbachev's Kremlin* (1992, Pantheon).

Morrison, John, *Boris Yeltsin: From Bolshevik to Democrat* (1991, Penguin).
A relatively uncritical account, but the best general study of his career.

Shevardnadze, Eduard, *The Future Belongs to Freedom* (1991, Free Press).

Vaksberg, Arkady, *The Soviet Mafia* (1991, Weidenfeld & Nicolson).
A fascinating account of the corruption and lawlessness of the 1970s and 1980s from the personal perspective of one of the USSR's only genuine investigative journalists.

Yeltsin, Boris, *Against the Grain* (1990, Jonathan Cape).
Rather meandering, but necessary.

Studies of Specific Issues and Periods

Aslund, Anders, *Gorbachev's Struggle for Economic Reform* (1989, Pinter).

Brown, Archie, 'Andropov: discipline *and* reform', *Problems of Communism*, vol. 32, no. 1 (1983).

Brown, Archie, 'Gorbachev: new man in the Kremlin', *Problems of Communism*, vol. 34, no. 3 (1985).

Bushnell, John, *Moscow Graffiti* (1990, Unwin Hyman).
A brilliant anthropological study of the unofficial youth culture of the time.

Clark, William A., *Crime and Punishment in Soviet Officialdom* (1993, M. E. Sharpe).
A useful study of the corruption which had taken such a powerful grip of the Soviet elite by Gorbachev's time.

Dallinn, Alexander and Lapidus, Gail (eds.), *The Soviet System in Crisis* (1991, Westview).
A reader of many of the most useful and insightful articles written about the Gorbachev era and contemporary Soviet writings.

Dawisha, Karen, *Eastern Europe, Gorbachev and Reform* (1990, Cambridge University Press).

Galeotti, Mark, *The Age of Anxiety: Security and Politics in Soviet and post-Soviet Russia* (1995, Longman).
The story of the era, very much framed in terms of security issues.

Hill, Ronald and Frank, Peter, *The Soviet Communist Party* (1986, Allen & Unwin).

Knight, Amy, *The KGB* (1990, Unwin Hyman).
The best general study of the KGB since Stalin's era.

Lane, David (ed.), *Elites and Political Power in the USSR* (1988, Edward Elgar).

Lewin, Moshe, *The Gorbachev Phenomenon: A Historical Interpretation* (1988, University of California Press).

Smith, Graham (ed.), *The Nationalities Question in the Soviet Union* (1990, Longman).

Wilson, Andrew and Bachkatov, Nina, *Living with Glasnost* (1988, Penguin).

Zaslavskaya, Tatyana, 'The Novosibirsk report', *Survey*, vol. 28, no. 1 (1984). A report which helped shape the views of Gorbachev and many of his team.

INDEX

Index

XIX Party Conference (1988),
82–3, 89–93, 96
XXVII Party Congress (1986),
53, 65, 77
XXVIII Party Congress (1990),
113
Congress of People's Deputies,
90–3, 95, 97, 101–2
constitution, 4, 6, 91, 97
co-operatives, 75–6, *see also*
economy, and reform
corruption, 13, 25, 26, 29, 47, 55,
57, 68, 76, 79, *see also* anti-
corruption campaigns
Cossacks, 2
Czechoslovakia, 21, 45, 101

defence industries, 15–16, 115
Defence Ministry, *see* armed forces
democratization, 47, 66–7, 70, 84,
87–98, 99–100, 101–4, 106–7
dissidents, 25, 42
Duma, 85

economy, 14–18, 28, 31–2, 55–7,
58, 59, 70, 75–7, 80, 85–6, 95, 101
and reform, 38, 47, 55–7, 63–4,
75–7, 80, 85–6, 106, 108
elite, 4, 6–14, 17, 18, 21–2, 28–30,
39–40, 43–4, 52–4, 55, 63–4,
66–7, 68–9, 76, 79–81, 85–6, 95,
115
environmentalism, 67, 74
Estonia, 1, 113–14

Fedorchuk, Vitali, 27, 30
Finland, 23
foreign policy, 16, 47, 59–62, 77–8,
107
France, 7, 45

Gamsakhurdia, Zviad, 100
Georgia, 1, 21, 26, 53, 100, 113–14
German Democratic Republic (East
Germany), 21, 101

German Federal Republic (West
Germany/Unified Germany), 42,
45, 107
GKChP, *see* August Coup
glasnost', 54, 65, 67–73, 74–5, 82–3,
84, 88, 91, 98
Gorbachev, Mikhail, 3, 13–14, 28,
38–9, 40, 41, 42, 43–50, 51,
52–64, 65–83, 84–103, 105–24,
125–9, 130–1
his background and career,
30–3, 43–9, 125–9, 130–1
comparisons and assessments,
29, 55, 81, 120–4
his ideas, 45, 47–8, 52, 58, 60,
65–6, 68–73, 74, 82, 84, 86,
87–9, 101–3, 105, 107–12, 120,
122
and Yeltsin, 63, 75, 81–2,
102–3, 105, 111, 115, 120
Gorbacheva, Raisa, 44, 45, 122,
131
Gosplan, 16–17, 55–6, 80
gospriemka, 56–7
Grishin, Viktor, 48–9, 121, 131
Gromov, Boris, 108, 131
Gromyko, Andrei, 28, 39–40, 49,
50, 53, 60, 131

health, 58–9, 90
Hitler, 3
Hungary, 23–4

'informals', 73–5, 83, 88, 98
Interior Ministry, *see* MVD
Inter-Regional Group of Deputies,
97, 98
Iran, 20
Islam, 1, 19, 20, 82
Italian Communist Party (PCI),
46–7
Italy, 45, 46–7

Japan, 7, 85
Jews, 25, 27